A Designer's Guide to Period Style

A Designer's Guide to Period Style

Architecture, Décor, Furniture, and Costume from the Ancient World to the 19th Century

Kathleen Donnelly
University of Wisconsin Oshkosh

Roy Hoglund
University of Wisconsin Oshkosh

WAVELAND
PRESS, INC.

Long Grove, Illinois

For information about this book, contact:
Waveland Press, Inc.
4180 IL Route 83, Suite 101
Long Grove, Illinois 60047-9580
(847) 634-0081
info@waveland.com
www.waveland.com

CONTENTS

The idea for this book came from years of team-teaching the History of Styles course at the University of Wisconsin Oshkosh. As instructors in the design and technology area, we found that students studying design for the stage had little, if any, previous knowledge of styles in architecture and fashion, and a very limited vocabulary in these areas. This became very problematic when designing period productions, whether realized or as class projects. For this reason, we created the History of Styles class over twenty years ago to give students a basic understanding of styles throughout the ages. Through the teaching of this class, it became apparent that the teaching of visual styles required us to break down each style into its basic visual elements and to place that style in a logical timeline.

Although the class has been fine-tuned over the decades into an online format, there was still no textbook or reference guide available that covered the areas of architecture, décor, furniture, fashion, and accessories that related to our classroom approach. The purpose of this book is to illustrate the evolution of style from antiquity through the end of the 19th century, focusing primarily on Western style, with the goal to develop in the user an understanding of the "visual essence" of a given style. The visual essence had to be simplified into line and shape. Once the student is able to understand the relationship between the line and shape of a style, it becomes easier for them to transfer this visual knowledge to their own designs.

The visual essence in clothing more specifically relates to the silhouette created when the garment is worn on the body, along with the underpinnings that support and reshape the body. This silhouette can be vertical or horizontal in appearance depending on the intention of the style. Items such as hats, hair styles, or accessories often aid in creating the desired silhouette. This can also be true with architecture, furniture, and décor in which some styles attempt to stress the vertical or horizontal nature of a structure or object and use elements that make up the structure to help create that overall appearance.

For example, the Gothic style in architecture attempted to create a vertical appearance, drawing one's eye and focus upward. This attempt at a vertical appearance in the Gothic style is opposite to the Renaissance style in architecture which used classical elements such as columns, capitals, and decoration along with mathematical balance to give a symmetrical harmony to the appearance of the structure. Similar to architecture, the clothing in the Gothic period also stressed a vertical silhouette as garments were girdled on the hip, creating the illusion of an elongated body. In contrast, the Tudor period of the late Renaissance, with its square neckline and boxy style, stressed an intentional horizontal silhouette for both women and men.

Drawings of clothing, accessories, architecture, décor, and furniture, along with brief explanations, comprise the body of the book. The book is organized by chapters in chronological order, and because we have included the areas of fashion and architecture within each chapter, we have attempted to simplify the dates of various periods and styles. These are not hard and fast dates, but instead an estimate of dates within a timeline to better understand the style and its relationship in time.

Illustrations have been created by the authors, and were inspired by primary research for the time period to provide the most accurate portrayal of the lines and silhouette. The illustrations in this book are intended to clearly articulate the silhouettes and the elements used to accentuate and create the style as we know it. Its intention is to introduce or remind users of the basic silhouettes and elements that comprise various styles throughout the ages. It is not considered a history book, but instead a reference guide for those who design or reproduce work from historical styles.

We hope that you enjoy this book, whether as a designer or historian, and gain appreciation of the evolution of period styles.

Kathleen Donnelly and Roy Hoglund
July 2020

ACKNOWLEDGMENTS

We want to acknowledge the support we received from the Faculty Development Program at the University of Wisconsin Oshkosh during the development of this book. We wish to express our gratitude to Don Rosso and Waveland Press, for their guidance and support in the publication of this book, and to Pat Mackay and the late Ralph Pine who initially encouraged us to embark on this project. Special thanks to Paula Hoglund for her editorial and writing guidance. And finally, to all of our past students from the History of Styles class, who inspired and encouraged us to create this book, we thank you.

Classical Period

This period consists of styles from ancient Egypt, Greece, and Roman cultures. Although each contributes design elements that have influenced other cultures throughout history, you will also notice similarities or recurring visual themes between these three cultures, as well as materials and design elements which are uniquely their own. The Egyptians' belief in the afterlife has provided us with a wealth of information about their lives, customs, clothing, and architecture. Our foundation in rhetoric, democracy, and theater originate in ancient Greece. The pyramids in Ancient Egypt and the aqueducts in Rome exemplify their abilities in the field of engineering. Many of these edifices are still standing as a reminder of their greatness.

Architecture / Furniture / Décor

In all three of these cultures, local plants, animals, and symbols were incorporated into the styles that were developed. The Egyptians incorporated papyrus, lotus, and palm plants into the designs of their columns and capitals as well as vulture, lion, and the orb elements. The Greek and Romans also used stylized local plant life, such as the acanthus leaf, as well as animal legs and feet into their design elements for columns, capitals, and furniture. In all instances, although starting out as bold elements, they became subtle influences over time.

Costume

The wall paintings, statues, jewelry, and artifacts excavated from the pyramids in Ancient Egypt provide us with detailed information on the style and silhouette of clothing and accessories, as well as color and pattern. Much of our information about Greek clothing can be found in statues and painted vases that illustrate scenes from the life of the Greeks as well as the gods and goddesses. When the Romans conquered Greece, they adopted many of the styles of Greece as a basis for their own. Roman mosaics and coins, in addition to statues and architectural reliefs, provide information about clothing. All three cultures used wool and linen as the primary fabrics, with dyes extracted from nature.

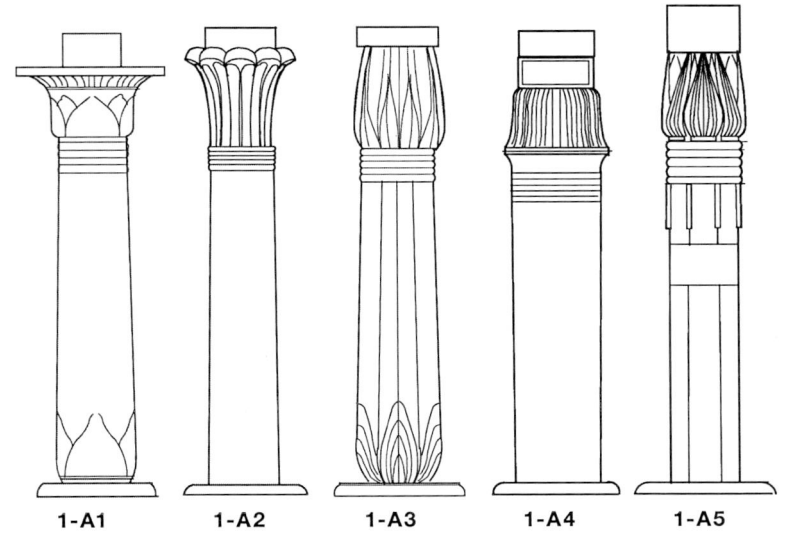

1-A1   1-A2   1-A3   1-A4   1-A5

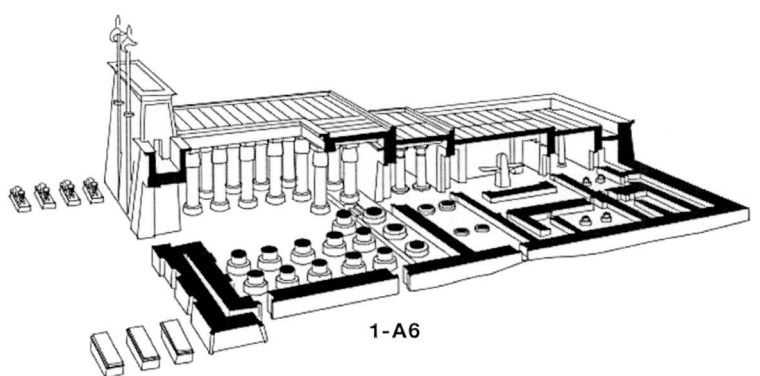

1-A6

1-A1   EGYPTIAN — LOTUS BUNDLE COLUMN
Thebes

1-A2   EGYPTIAN — PALM FAN COLUMN
Thebes

1-A3   EGYPTIAN — PAPYRUS CLUSTER COLUMN WITH BUD CAPITAL
Thebes

1-A4   EGYPTIAN — TENT POLE COLUMN
Temple of Thutmose III, Karnak

1-A5   EGYPTIAN — LOTUS BUNDLE COLUMN
Thebes

1-A6   EGYPTIAN — TEMPLE OF KARNAK
A temple complex which was added onto over a thousand years includes temples, pylons, and chapels. 1550–323 BCE.

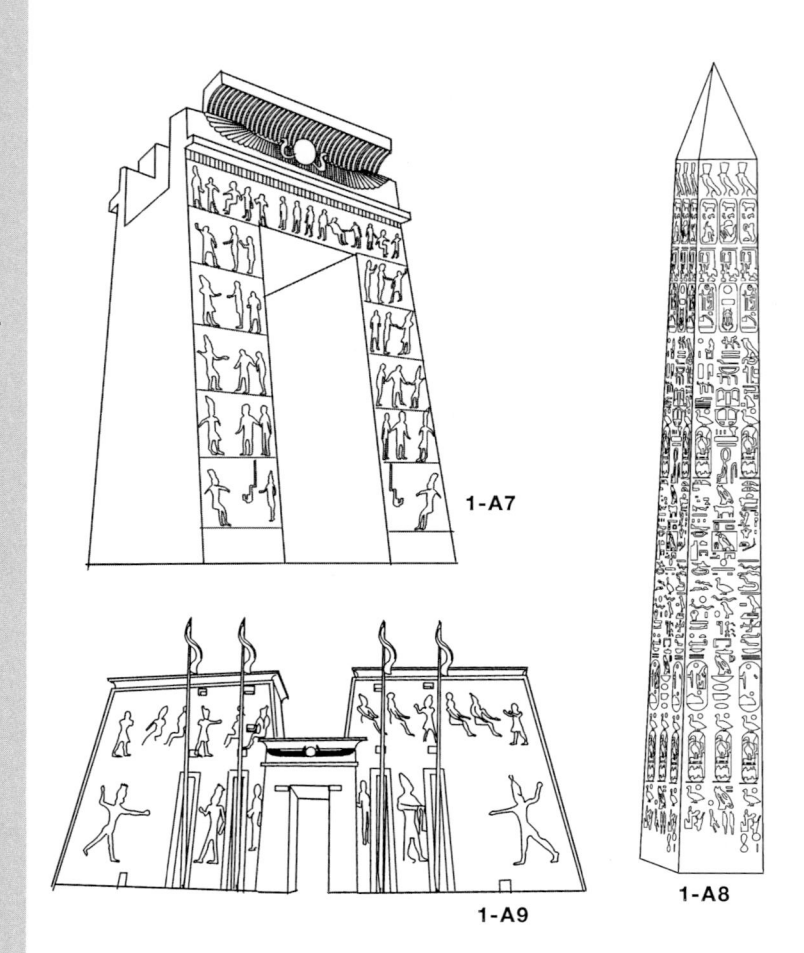

1-A7

1-A8

1-A9

1-A7 EGYPTIAN — GATE OF PTOLEMY III
Located in the temple of Karnak with images of the vulture, wings, cobra, and orb. 18th Dynasty.

1-A8 EGYPTIAN — OBELISK OF THUTMOSE III
Also known as Cleopatra's Needle, one of a pair of obelisks originally located in Heliopolis. 1450 BCE.

1-A9 EGYPTIAN — THE MAIN PYLON OF THE TEMPLE OF KARNAK
The walls are sloping, which makes the base larger than the top. Low-relief hieroglyphics are carved and painted into the surface, illustrating the king's authority. Four niches are created to hold flagpoles. Originally four large statues were in front of this structure. A pronounced cornice caps off the top of the façade. Between 237 BCE and 57 BCE.

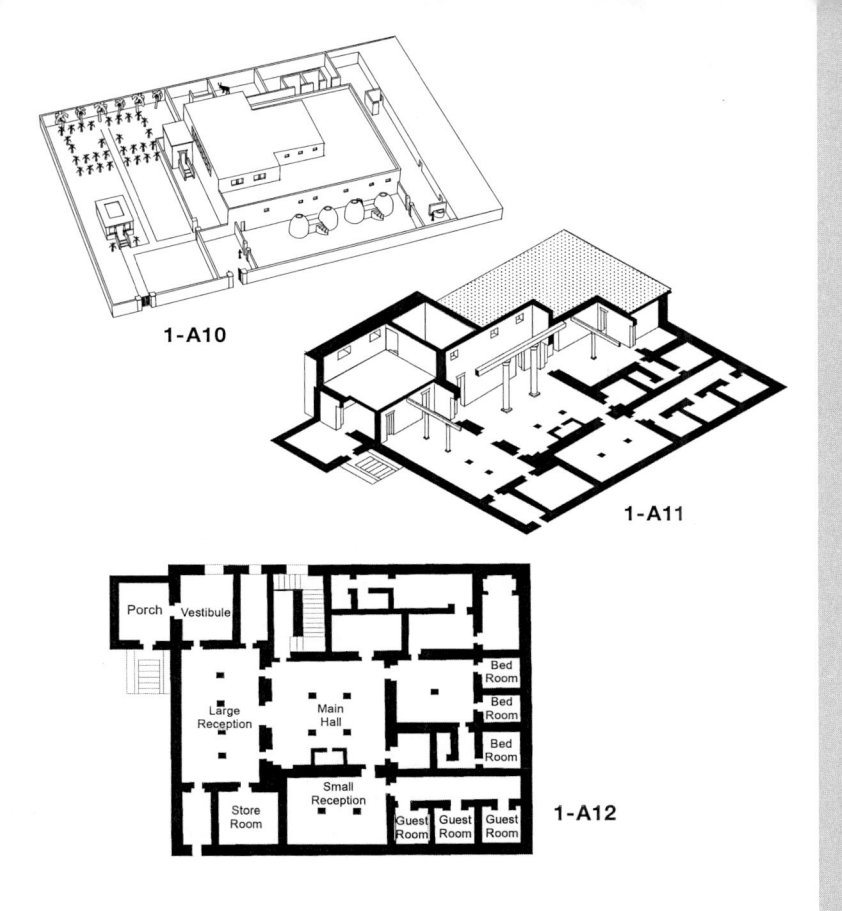

1-A10

1-A11

1-A12

1-A10   EGYPTIAN — HOUSE IN AMARNA
Here the entire layout of the grounds can be seen, including the gardens, temple, outside ovens, and servants' quarters. Walls surround the entire complex. Amarna, New Kingdom.

1-A11   EGYPTIAN — HOUSE INTERNAL VIEW
This cutaway of the house illustrates the multiple levels used, with post and lintel support for the ceiling. Windows were generally small and high up on the wall for the first floor, and open verandas were used on the second floor. Amarna, New Kingdom.

1-A12   EGYPTIAN — GROUND PLAN OF HOUSE IN AMARNA
This is a ground plan of a villa. There is a main entrance and a vestibule or waiting room. Large and small rooms were used for ceremonies and entertainment; smaller rooms were used for bedrooms and storage. Cooking was either in an uncovered room or outside. Servants and courtiers were typically separated from the main house. The houses were generally made from mud bricks with wood beam ceilings. Windows were clerestory, and stairs were used to access an upper floor and the roof. Second floors were also used as living spaces. Amarna, New Kingdom.

1-A13   1-A14   1-A15   1-A16

1-A13   GREEK — DORIC COLUMN
Usually wider than Ionic or Corinthian, it has a more pronounced shape with a simple capital or echinus and sharp fluting.

1-A14   GREEK — IONIC COLUMN
Usually taller than Doric, possessing a scroll-top capital, with a column base and flat-edged fluting on the shaft.

1-A15   GREEK — CORINTHIAN COLUMN
Similar to Ionic, but with a capital that incorporates acanthus leaves and minor scrolls.

1-A16   GREEK — CARYATID COLUMN
Used in the Hellenistic period with carved figures which doubled as columns. Many times the capital functioned as a hat or crown on the figure.

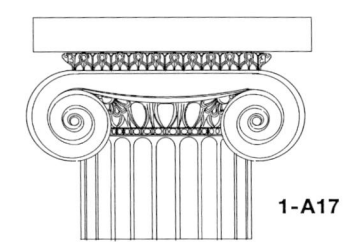

1-A17

1-A18

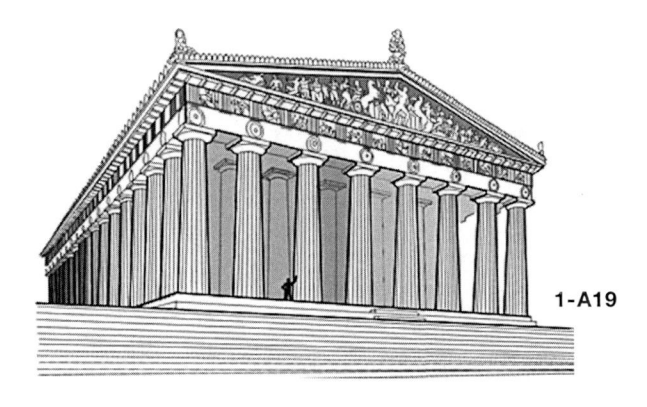

1-A19

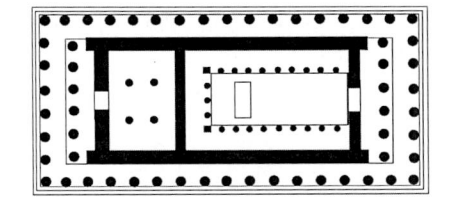

1-A20

1-A17 GREEK — DETAIL OF GREEK IONIC CAPITAL
The Ionic capital is an inverted scroll, with an egg and dart area between the scrolls.

1-A18 GREEK — DETAIL OF GREEK CORINTHIAN CAPITAL
The Corinthian capital consists mainly of stylized acanthus leaves and periodic rosettes.

1-A19 GREEK — PARTHENON
The pediment could have had carved figures in high relief in that space. These figures could also have been found in the entablature or space between the triglyphs in the frieze area of the roof beam ends. The straight roofline could also be broken up with acroterion decoration. 438 BCE.

1-A20 GREEK — PARTHENON GROUND PLAN
The typical Greek Doric temple was based on a rectangle with steps or stylobate surrounding the base. A single row of columns supported the roof which had a pediment on both short ends.

1-A21   GREEK — TEMPLE OF ARTEMIS AT EPHESUS

Much like Doric temples, Ionic temples would be based on the rectangle. Steps of the stylobate surrounded the base. Because Ionic columns were narrower than the Doric, additional columns could be included. The effect was to give a lighter, more delicate feel to the structure. Sometimes a drum or extended base was designed into the column decorated with low-relief figures. Dentils were many times included in the pediment cornice design. 550 BCE.

1-A22   GREEK — TEMPLE OF ARTEMIS GROUND PLAN

As shown in the ground plan, two rows of columns were used to support the roof. There was often a desire to more clearly distinguish a formal entrance into the temple when compared to the Doric model. Corinthian temples were very similar to the Ionic temples with the exception of the capitals, which used acanthus leaves in the design.

1-A23   GREEK — STOA OF ATTALOS

During the reign of Attalos II of Pergamon, a market building would consist of double colonnades and two stories providing 42 shops, with the lower half of the columns smooth to protect the fluting from damage by users. Stairs were located on the outside to access the second floor.

1-A24   GREEK — GROUND PLAN OF FIRST FLOOR, STOA OF ATTALOS

Covered walkways with marble columns supporting the upper floor were in ascending order, with Doric columns on the first floor and Ionic on the second floor.

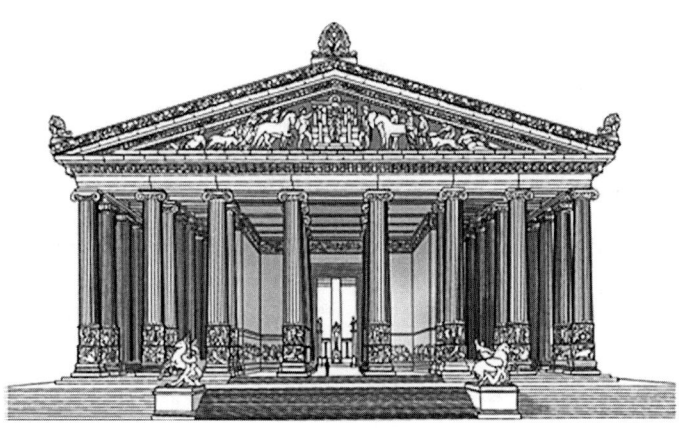

1-A21

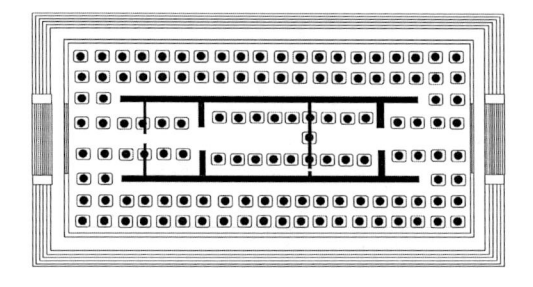

1-A22

1-A23

1-A24

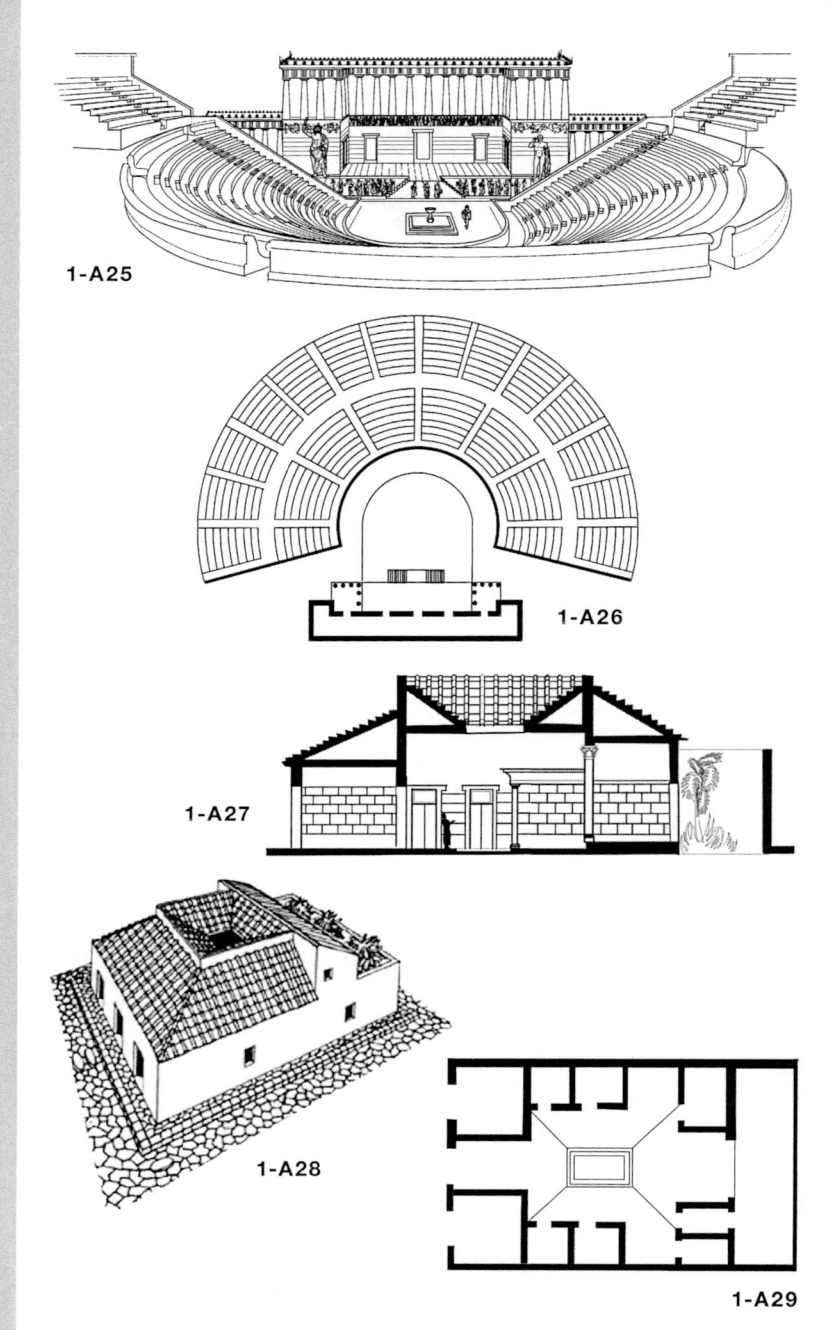

1-A25

1-A26

1-A27

1-A28

1-A29

1-A25 GREEK — THEATER AT SEGESTA
Designed to hold 4,000 people, this theater has an altar in the center, and a low retaining wall around the orchestra. The proscenium could be accessed by steps from the orchestra level. The upper level was surrounded by a colonnade. The skene was once decorated with images to the god Pan. Late 4th to the early 3rd century BCE.

1-A30

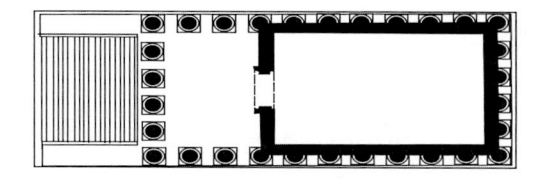

1-A31

1-A26   GREEK – GROUND PLAN OF THE THEATER AT SEGESTA
The seating was carved out of the local hillside and could hold 4,000. The parados, or chorus entrance avenues, could also be backed by a colonnade or similar structure in the Greek Doric style.

1-A27   GREEK – SECTION OF A GREEK ATRIUM HOUSE
The center, or atrium area of the house, was open to the sky. A small garden could be located at the back of the house.

1-A28   GREEK – SKETCH OF A GREEK ATRIUM HOUSE
Walls were stucco on the outside with clay tile roofs.

1-A29   GREEK – GROUND PLAN OF A GREEK ATRIUM HOUSE
To enter into the house, one first went through a vestibule before getting to the atrium area.

1-A30   ROMAN – MAISON CARRÉE IN NÎMES
Maison Carrée is considered a typical style of a Roman temple. Unlike Greek temples, Roman temples had a main entrance as seen by the pillared portico to the left of the structure. There was one main set of doors with Corinthian columns surrounding the structure. 4 CE.

1-A31   ROMAN – MAISON CARRÉE GROUND PLAN
The temple ground plan pictured here is a rectangle about twice as long as its width. Steps are found on just one side. The pediment which overhangs the entrance takes up about one-third of the overall length of the space.

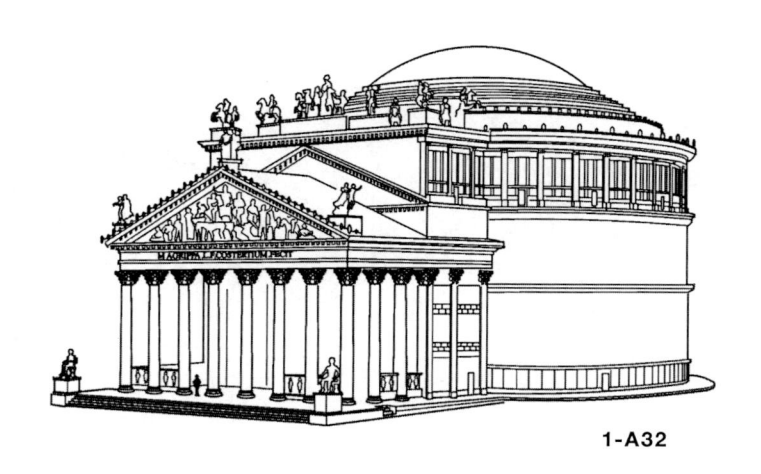

1-A32

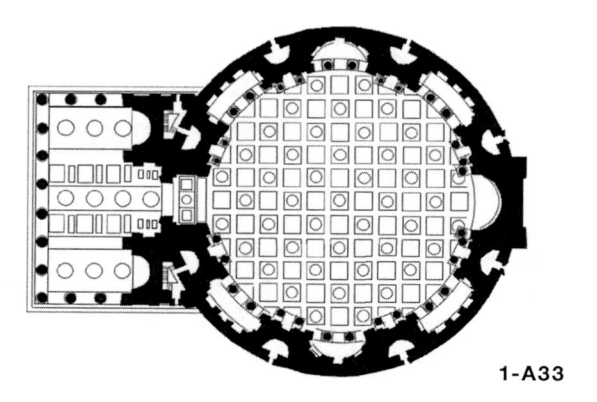

1-A33

1-A32   ROMAN — PANTHEON IN ROME

The Pantheon is a later version of a Roman temple. It, too, has a pillared portico that accentuates the main entrance. The columns have Corinthian capitals. In its original state, it had many reliefs and statues decorating the outside of the building.126 CE.

1-A33   ROMAN — PANTHEON GROUND PLAN

The main body of the building is a round drum with a portico on the front. This drum has a coffered, domed ceiling with various niches around the interior walls.

1-A34   ROMAN — PANTHEON SECTION VIEW

Because Rome had become experts in the use of concrete, they were able to develop a domed coffered ceiling which covered the entire drum. In the center of the drum is a round opening called an oculus that allows sunlight to enter the interior of the space. The original structure was to be a temple to all of the gods. For this reason, many niches exist on the inside of the building.

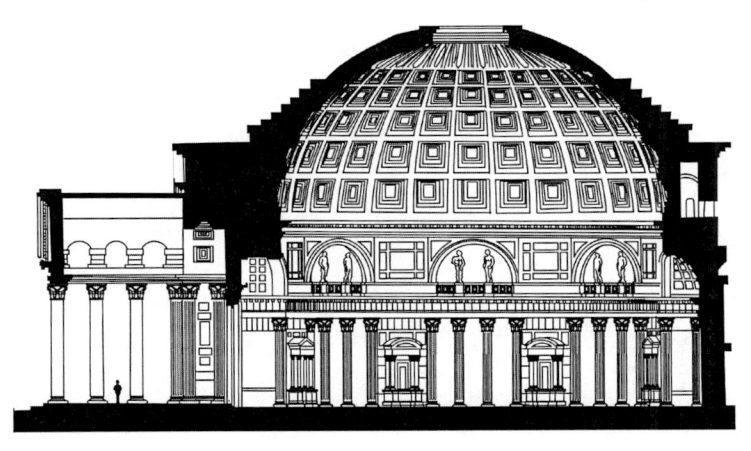

1-A34

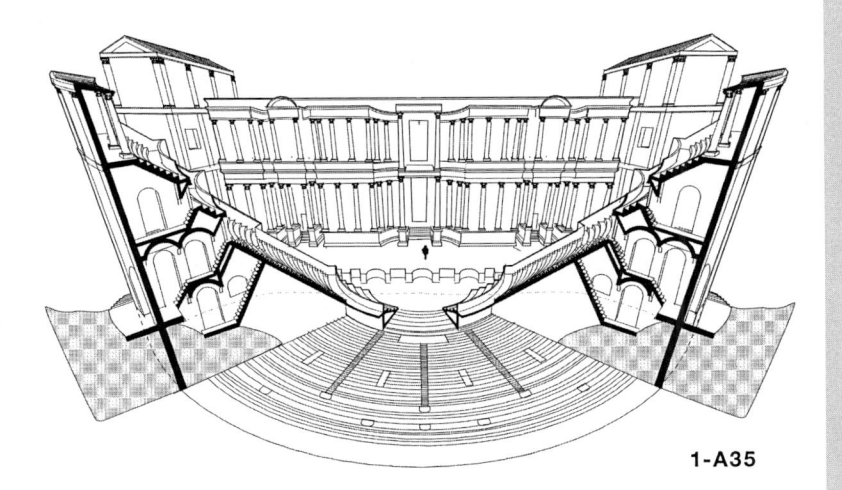

1-A35

1-A35   ROMAN — THEATRE OF MÉRIDA

Unlike other theaters in the Roman Empire that were built on level ground, the Roman Theatre of Mérida in Spain, was built into the side of the San Albin hill. The stage, and seating area which had a steep rake, created a surround around the orchestra area. Background for the stage is two stories of elaborate architectural elements. Poles around the periphery were used to support a tarp to keep out the sun and elements. The theater could hold an audience of 6,000. 16 BCE.

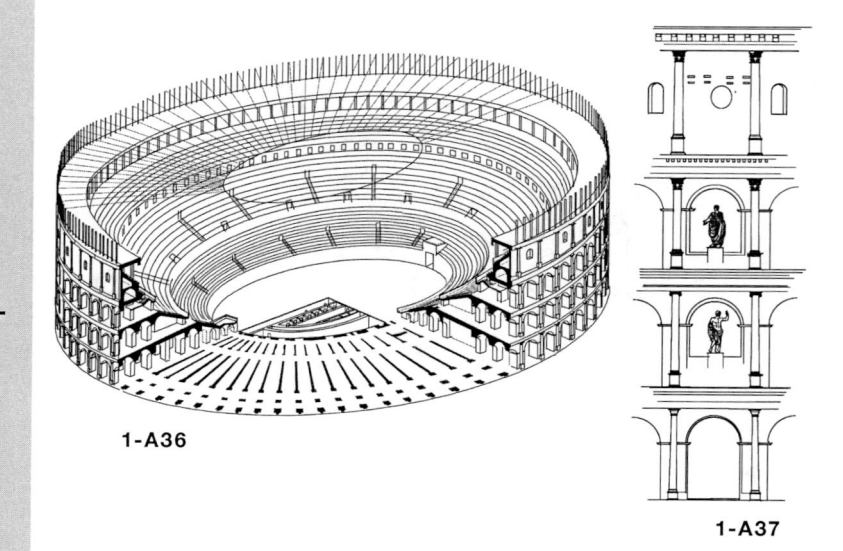

1-A36

1-A37

1-A36 ROME — FLAVIAN AMPHITHEATER, COLOSSEUM

An elliptical plan with seats rising from a retaining wall up to the highest level holding 50,000 spectators. This Roman landmark, known to most people today as the Colosseum, was built during the Flavian dynasty. The use of the arch is employed consistently throughout the structure. At one time it had been covered with a veneer of marble. Stairs and ramps allowed spectators to enter and exit the structure quickly. It also enabled gladiators to enter and exit the structure through different passages. In later renovations the area beneath the amphitheater floor was reconstructed creating passages, rooms for animals and gladiators, and trap doors with elevators to raise or lower people from the playing area. 80 CE.

1-A37 ROMAN — FLAVIAN AMPHITHEATER, EXTERIOR DETAILS

An ascending order of style was engaged in the design used on the outside of the structure. Tuscan order columns were used on the lowest level with Ionic order used on the second level. The third level consisted of the Corinthian style. This style was also used on the pilasters of the upper level. Statues of various emperors filled arched openings.

1-A38 ROMAN — PERISTYLE HOUSE

Small windows and thick walls are typical on the outside of the house. Roofs are ceramic tile, directing water into both the atrium and the peristyle. The peristyle is the columned courtyard near the rear of the house. Roman houses could be two stories high. Many houses in communities have shops around the outside, sharing a common wall with the house itself.

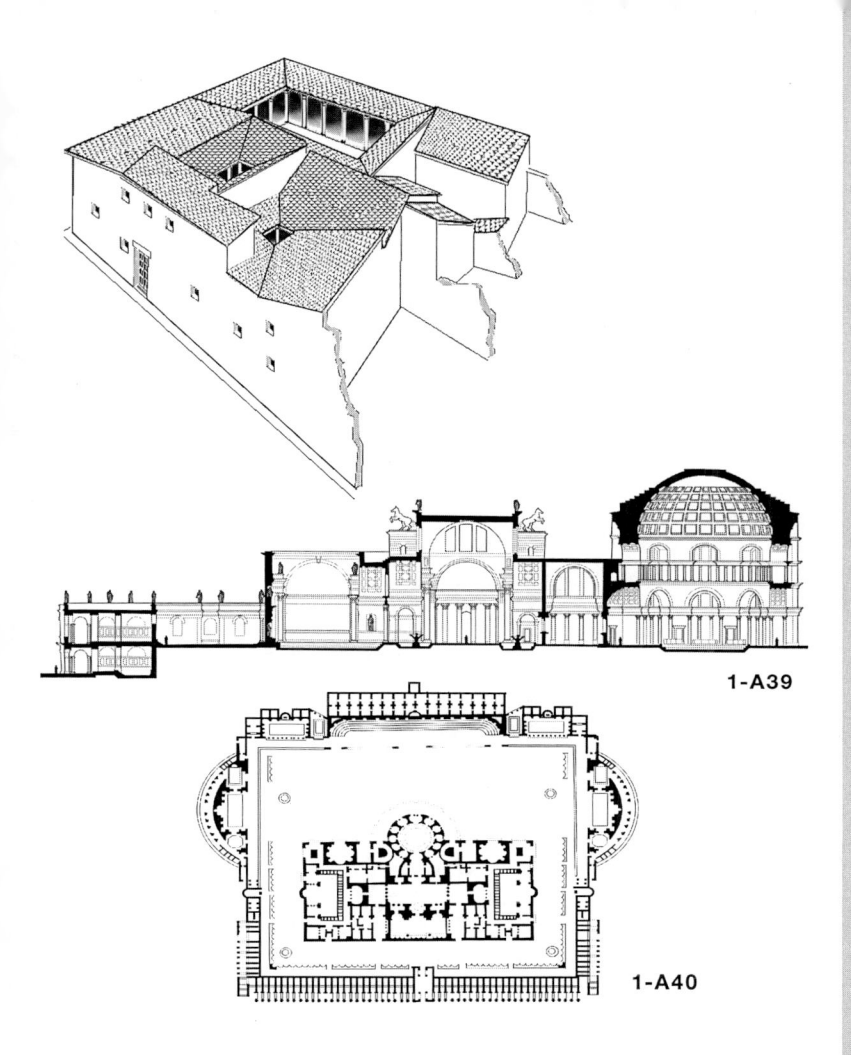

1-A39

1-A40

1-A39   ROMAN — BATHS AT CARACALLA

Roman Baths were public structures for social, business, and politics. They were generally large complexes with baths of hot and cold water, swimming pools, gyms for wrestling, steam rooms, and theaters, as well as shops which sold a variety of items. All of the Roman construction techniques and designs were engaged. Domed pool areas, vaulted and coffered ceilings, and large open areas made up the complex. Water was supplied through aqueducts and heated through ceramic piping beneath the floors. The Baths at Caracalla could accommodate 1,600 bathers. 35 CE.

1-A40   ROMAN — BATHS AT CARACALLA GROUND PLAN

The Baths at Caracalla covered an area of 1/5 of a mile square; shops were located outside of the surrounding wall.

1-A41

1-A42

1-A41 ROMAN — TRIUMPHAL ARCH OF CONSTANTINE

Created as a monument to the military successes of Emperor Constantine, this triumphal arch consists of three archways. Corinthian columns flank each archway with a Corinthian pilaster behind. Low-relief panels reflecting battle scenes decorate all sides of the arch. An ornate cornice with brackets sits above the columns with statues of prisoners at the very top. Much of the marble and decorative panels and statues come from other arches in Rome. 312 CE.

1-A42 ROMAN — AQUEDUCT OF SEGOVIA IN SPAIN

Masonry arches were constructed to allow water to be brought into Rome and other cities across valleys. These passages, although intended to be used for water, also doubled as bridges. This enabled water from mountain reservoirs to be brought to cities over great distances. Pipes of ceramic and lead were created to guide the water. The archways were constructed to allow for a gradual downward slope, enabling gravity to move the water to its final location.

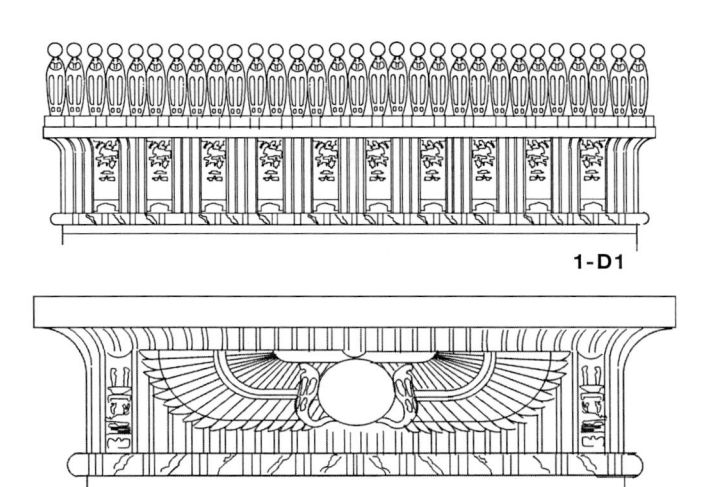

1-D1

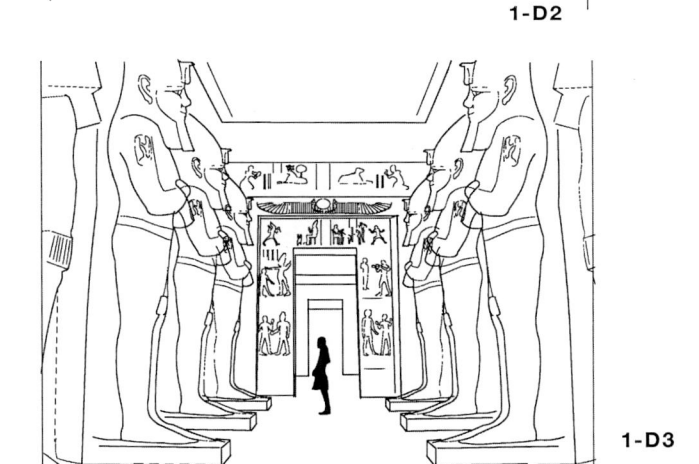

1-D2

1-D3

1-D1   EGYPTIAN — COBRA AND ORB CORNICE
Cornice decoration over entrances. Stylized cobras with the orb overhead are used as a repeat, with smaller hieroglyphic designs repeated below. From the Temple of Kom Ombo. 180–47 BCE.

1-D2   EGYPTIAN — VULTURE, ORB, AND COBRA CORNICE
Interior cornice decoration over entrances could use stylized cobras with the orb overhead and repeated, with smaller hieroglyphic designs repeated below. Temple of Sobek, Kom Ombo. 180–47 BCE.

1-D3   EGYPTIAN — TEMPLE OF ABU SIMBEL
Eight statues of Ramses II are attached to columns that support the ceiling. Decorations include hieroglyphics depicting Ramses' successes in battle. 1264–1224 BCE.

1-D4

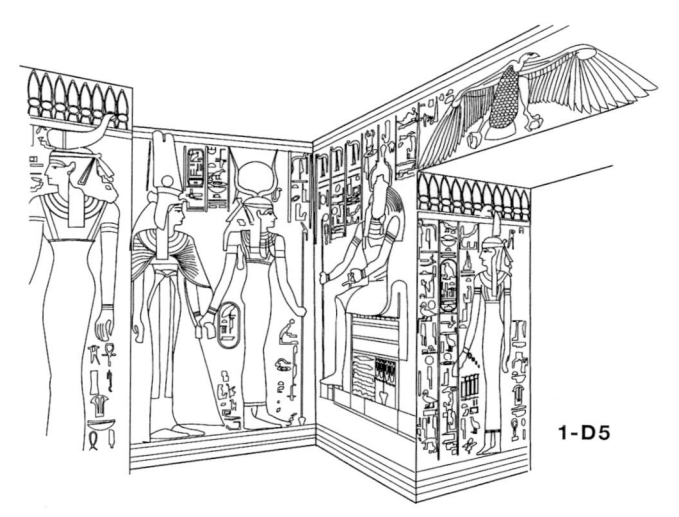

1-D5

1-D4 EGYPTIAN – TEMPLE OF KARNAK

The Great Hypostyle Hall in the Temple of Karnak is part of the Temple complex. The center nave is supported by 12 open papyrus flower columns. On either side of the nave, 122 smaller closed-bud papyrus columns support an architrave roof. Large clerestory windows with stone grates are located on either side of the taller nave area. The columns and interior walls are decorated with low-relief and painted hieroglyphics. Constructed between 237 BCE and 57 BCE.

1-D5 EGYPTIAN – TOMB OF QUEEN NEFERTARI

Hieroglyphic wall paintings include a lightly painted border top and bottom with royal figures and deities in large scale. Smaller figures and hieroglyphics are spaced around these figures. Stylized cobra and vultures cap off some walls and entrance areas. 1295–1255 BCE.

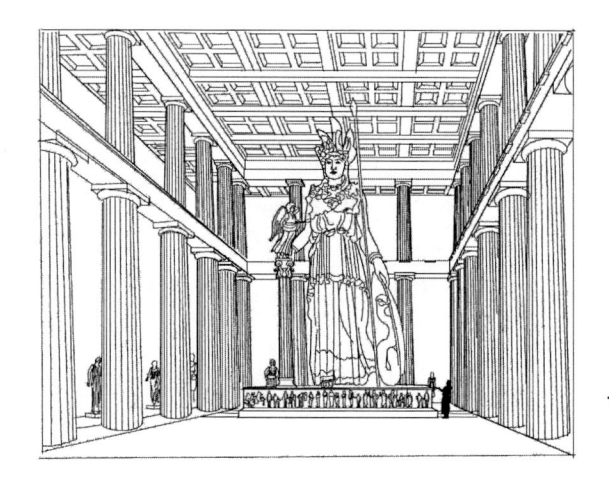

1-D6

1-D7

1-D6   GREEK — INTERIOR OF THE PARTHENON

On the interior or cella of the Parthenon was a large statue of
Athena standing almost 38 feet tall. It was placed in a peristyle of
Doric columns. A reflecting pool was created in front of the statue
which reflected light on the statue and into the rest of the room. It
also generated moisture to help preserve the statue. Completed in
438 BCE, it has long since disappeared.

1-D7   DETAILS OF THE GODDESS ATHENA

The statue was made of ivory for the flesh areas and gold for
the other areas, all placed on a wood superstructure. Athena
is dressed in warrior fashion with a spear and shield along with
a helmet and breastplate. A smaller statue of Nike stands in
Athena's right hand.

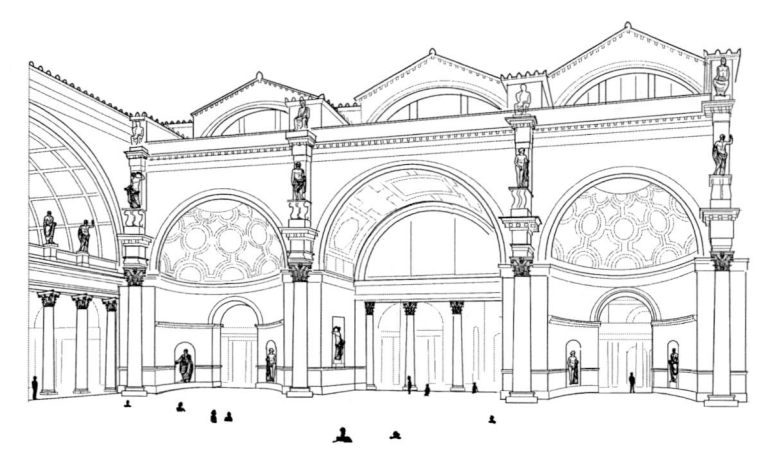

1-D8

1-D9

1-D8   ROMAN — BATHS OF CARACALLA

Although this example illustrates an open air pool, it has a number
of features used in the interior designs. Vaulted or domed ceilings
usually have a coffered design incorporated into it. Roman lattice
is used in window openings and for railings. Niches for the statues
of important dignitaries and columns used to create supports
and pedestals for statues are also part of the design. The pool
pictured here is the Frigidarium. 235 CE.

1-D10

1-D11

1-D12

1-D9   ROMAN — INTERIOR OF A PERISTYLE HOUSE
There are similarities between Greek and Roman houses. This image illustrates the atrium of this house just beyond the vestibule or entrance. The opening in the ceiling allows light as well as rain water which collects in the impluvium or floor basin. From the tablinum or dining area, you can see through to the peristylium or court area. Floors may be stone tiled or mosaic; walls may have a veneer of marble or granite or have a wall painting done in an early fresco technique. Ceilings would have been wood beamed and may have had wood coffers in the ceiling areas in between the beams. Rooms would have been located off of the atrium and may have had Roman lattice in the transom area. Statues of gods or past relatives may also have been incorporated into the room.

1-D10   ROMAN — FIRST PHASE OF ROMAN WALL PAINTING
This style would have been intended to replicate marble, granite, or some type of exotic material. Usually painted into wet plaster.

1-D11   ROMAN — SECOND PHASE OF ROMAN WALL PAINTING
This style used architecture to create vistas with skewed perspective.

1-D12   ROMAN — THIRD PHASE OF ROMAN WALL PAINTING
In this ornate style, architecture is used to create picture frames in which images telling a story would be placed. In this way entire walls would be used to become a gallery of images and stories.

1-F1

1-F2

1-F4

1-F3

1-F5

1-F1   EGYPTIAN — SQUARE STOOL
Stool has a double cove seat. Supports could be square or rounded with diagonal supports. New Kingdom.

1-F2   EGYPTIAN — FOLDING STOOL
Stool has a seat made of animal hide. Many times, supports were carved to look like animals such as ducks. Middle Kingdom.

1-F3   EGYPTIAN — SMALL PANEL TOILET CABINET
Panels are set into support members; stretchers are located between the lower portion of the legs; diagonal supports help to stabilize the cabinet. Lids are either set in place or pinned to pivot to allow access to compartments. New Kingdom.

1-F4   EGYPTIAN — SMALL WOOD TABLE
Splayed legs, cove trim under the table top, and a single stretcher to stabilize the legs are part of the Egyptian style. Middle Kingdom.

1-F5   EGYPTIAN — HIGH BACKED THRONE
Made of wood, the chair was coated in white gesso, with low-relief images of the vulture and other hieroglyphic images carved in the back. Legs and feet are in the shape of a lion, decorative stabilizing elements connect to the stretcher bars between the legs, and the double cove seat are all Egyptian-style elements. 18th Egyptian Dynasty.

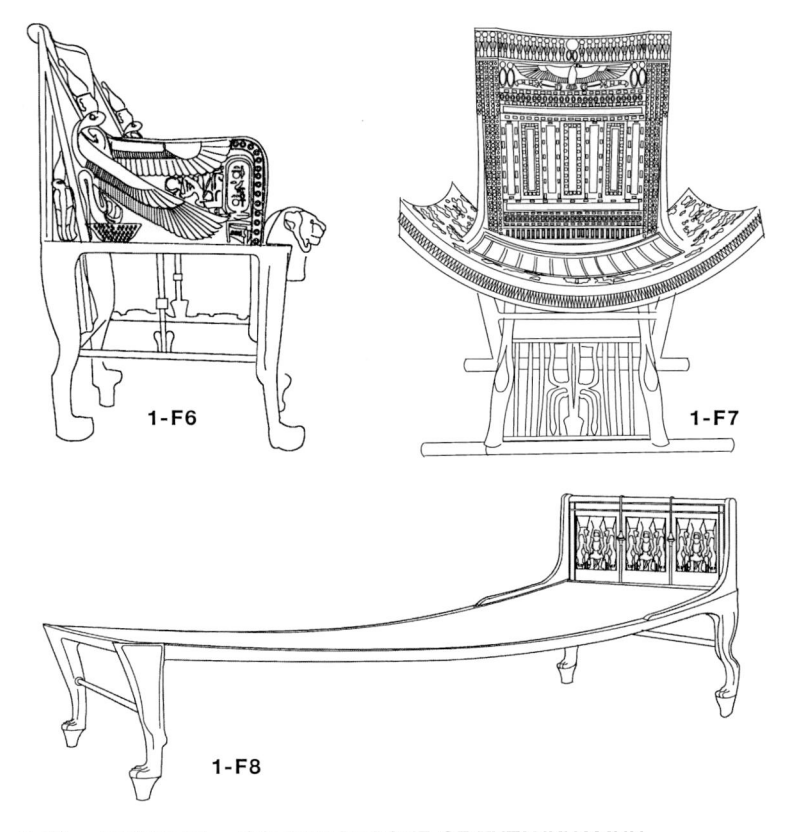

1-F6

1-F7

1-F8

1-F6 EGYPTIAN – GOLDEN THRONE OF TUTANKHAMUN

The throne is made of wood and covered in gold and silver. Inlays of semi-precious stones and glass are used to decorate the hieroglyphics in the design. Lions' legs and heads function as supports to the throne, and vulture wings are used as armrests.

1-F7 EGYPTIAN – THRONE OF TUTANKHAMUN

The Ceremonial Throne of Tutankhamun is made of wood. Although it appears to fold, it does not. It is constructed of ebony, covered in gold leaf, and inlaid with ivory, colored glass, and semi-precious stones. The seat is a double cove with decoration giving the appearance of an animal skin covering. The legs are a symbolic goose shape.

1-F8 EGYPTIAN – THE BED OF TUTANKHAMUN

Made of wood, the bed is covered in gold leaf, with cording woven across the frame of the bed. What appears to be the headboard is really the footboard with carved low relief. A head support would have been used instead of a pillow. Legs are carved in the likeness of a lion's legs. New Kingdom.

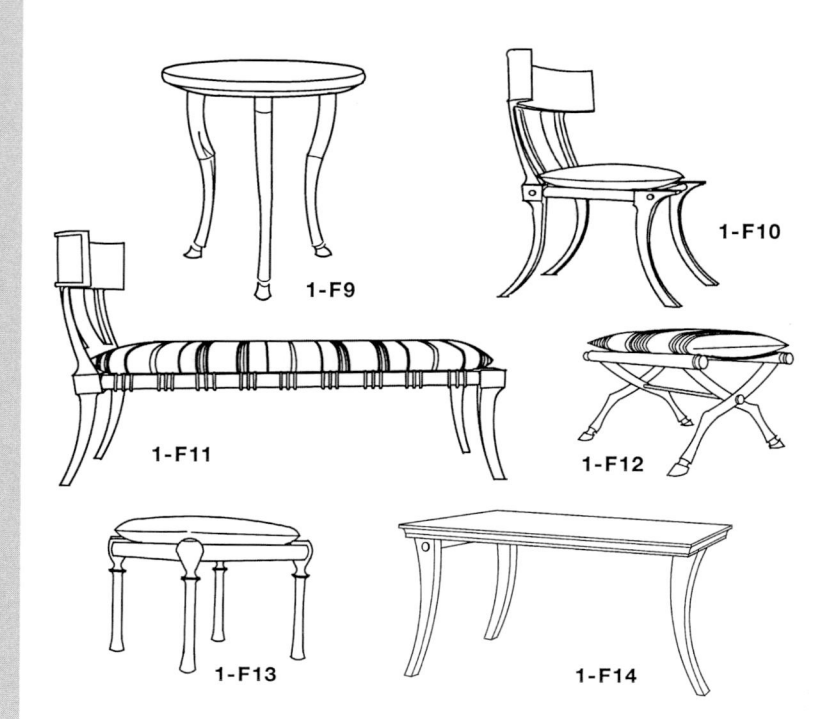

1-F9

1-F10

1-F11

1-F12

1-F13

1-F14

1-F9 GREEK — TABLE WITH THREE LEGS
Table is made of wood with supports shaped to look like deer legs. The table may have been used in conjunction with the kline or lounge.

1-F10 GREEK — KLISMOS CHAIR WITH PILLOW
This chair usually has sabre legs front and back with leather thong webbing to create a seat. Cushions are used over the leather for comfort. Typically these chairs would be made of wood.

1-F11 GREEK — KLISMOS COUCH WITH PILLOW
Klismos lounge or kline similar to the chair, it would have sabre legs front and back with a cushion over leather thong webbing. This piece of furniture would be used for reclining, eating, and sleeping.

1-F12 GREEK — FOLDING STOOL WITH PILLOW
Stool is designed to travel, legs are made in the shape of deer legs, and a cushion is used in addition to the webbing. Thought to be based on a military design.

1-F13 GREEK — SQUARE STOOL WITH TURNED LEGS AND PILLOW
The turned legs support a wood frame with leather thong webbing. A cushion is added to the webbing for comfort.

1-F14 GREEK — THREE-LEGGED RECTANGLE TABLE
Three sabre legs are used to support this rectangular table. Similar to the round table, it would be used in conjunction with the kline for dining.

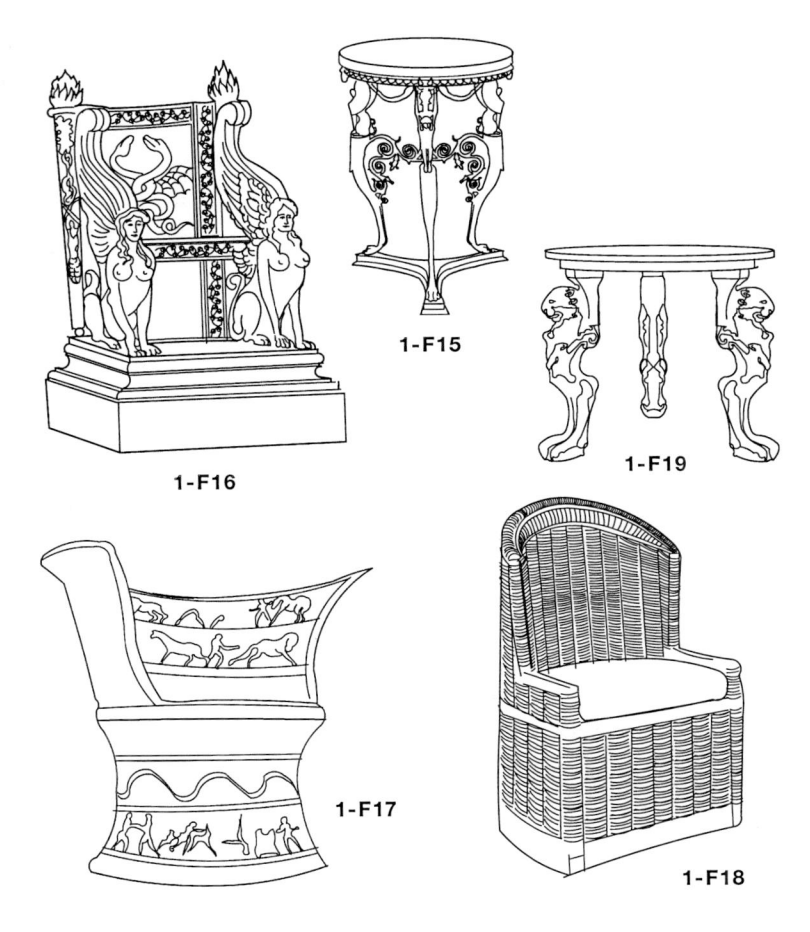

1-F15

1-F16

1-F19

1-F17

1-F18

1-F15   ROMAN — BRONZE TRIPOD TABLE
From the Temple of Isis, this table is made of bronze with sphinx
images seated on top of animal leg supports holding up the table
top. These types of supports could also hold a basin or a brazier.

1-F16   ROMAN — CHAIR OF STATE
This thronos is carved from a single block of marble. Images
include a sphinx whose wings become armrests. Torches
supporting the back represent knowledge.

1-F17   ROMAN — ROUND CHAIR
Chair is carved from marble with images that tell stories which are
carved in low relief into the back and base of the chair.

1-F18   ROMAN — WICKER CHAIR WITH PILLOW
Although this image is taken from a stone carving of this chair, it
represents the use of wicker in the Roman Empire for furniture. A
cushion would have been placed on the seat for comfort.

1-F19   ROMAN — ROUND TABLE
This table is carved out of marble and has legs that consist of a
lion's head mounted on top of a lion's rear leg.

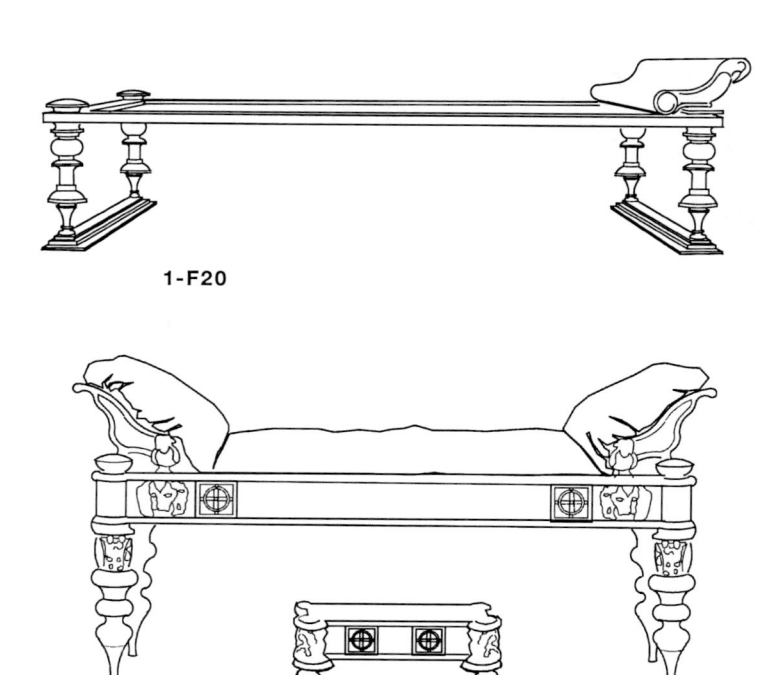

1-F20

1-F21

1-F20   ROMAN — BRONZE COUCH

This bronze couch was used for dining and sleeping. The turned legs were typical of Roman couches. The head of the couch had a fulcra or support for cushions and pillows which would be used on top of this piece of furniture. In this case, the image of a horse is incorporated into the design.

1-F21   ROMAN — IVORY COUCH AND FOOTREST

This couch has a fulcra on either side of the unit. It is constructed from ivory or bone with inlaid glass decoration. The ivory or bone pieces are turned and carved in images depicting the hunt. In addition, there are cupids and other mythical figures. Pillows and cushions are added for comfort.

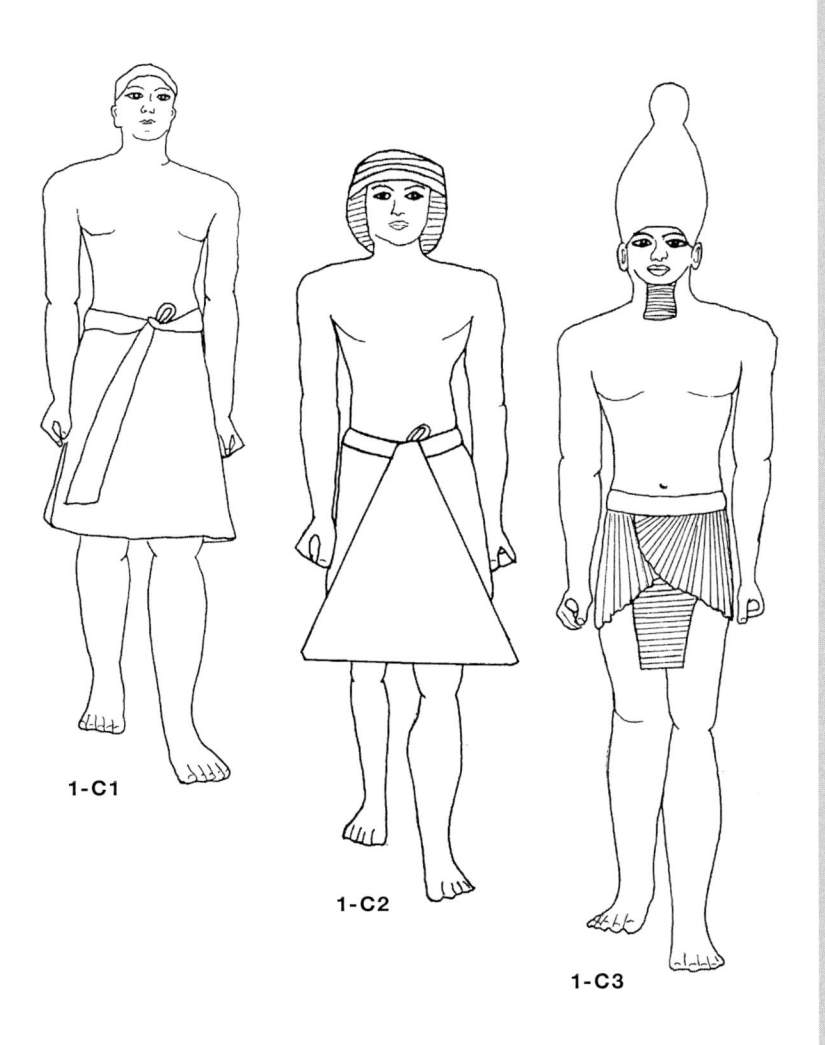

1-C1

1-C2

1-C3

1-C1 EGYPTIAN — LOIN SKIRT WITH BELT
The basic male garment wrapped around the body in a tubular fashion, and folded over the front. This was held together by a girdle/belt tied in a square knot.

1-C2 EGYPTIAN — LOIN SKIRT
In later years this could include a starched triangular piece of fabric in front to cover the genital area.

1-C3 EGYPTIAN — PLEATED SHENDYT KILT
This version of the male skirt was pleated and originally restricted to royalty. The fabric had two curved ends that joined in front and secured by a girdle/belt.

1-C4

1-C5

1-C6

1-C7

1-C4   EGYPTIAN — RED CROWN OF LOWER EGYPT
The red crown, also known as a Deshret crown, has a high back and lower flat crown in front. A wire, possibly a reed or leather, ending in a spiral extends toward the front of the headdress.

1-C5   EGYPTIAN — WHITE CROWN OF UPPER EGYPT
The white crown, also known as the Hedjet crown, is tall and in shape resembles a bowling pin. Historians believe the crown may be made of cloth or felt.

1-C6 & 1-C7   EGYPTIAN — PSCHENT, COMBINED CROWN OF UPPER AND LOWER EGYPT
When the upper and lower kingdoms in Egypt united, this headdress was fashioned as a combination of the physical elements of the individual crowns, along with the sacred uraeus (hooded cobra), which was placed in the center front of crown.

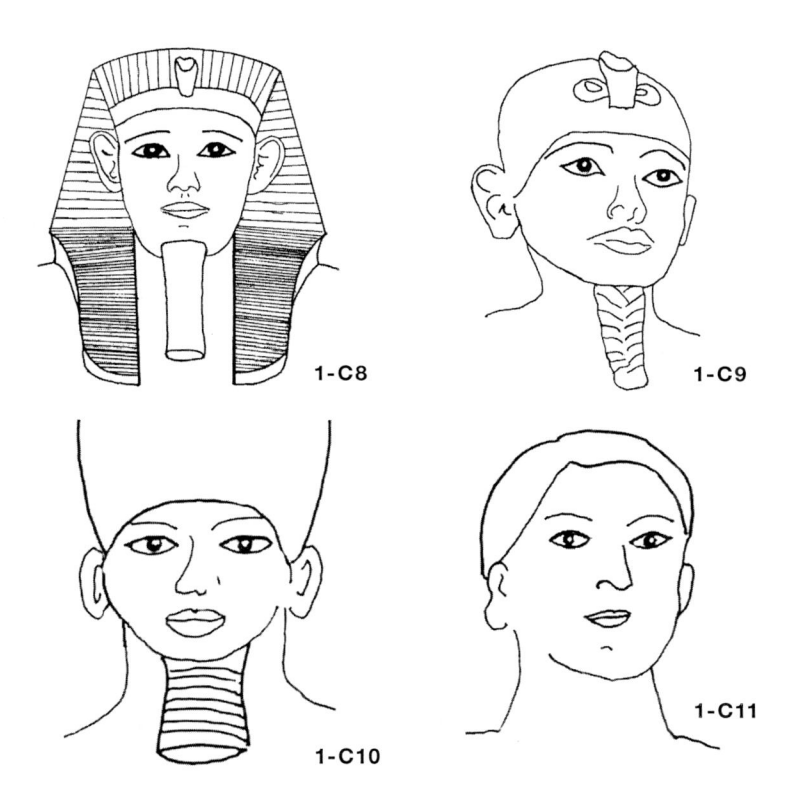

1-C8

1-C9

1-C11

1-C10

1-C8 EGYPTIAN — NEMES HEADDRESS AND POSTICHE (KING'S BEARD)

The Nemes headdress was made from a square piece of striped cloth that tied at the back of the head and carefully folded at the sides of the head, resembling the silhouette of the pyramids. There are three styles of false beards, known as postiche: God's beard (1-C9), King's beard (IC.8) and Noble beard (1-C10). Postiche was worn on formal or ceremonial occasions. The beards were knotted or plaited and hooked behind the ears.

1-C9 EGYPTIAN — CAP WITH SACRED URAEUS AND POSTICHE (GOD'S BEARD)

This is an example of a God's beard, which was longer and had a curled end. Only Emperors could wear this style of postiche.

1-C10 EGYPTIAN — POSTICHE (NOBILITY)

The last style of beard, which could be worn by men who were considered nobility or royalty, was shorter than the other two styles and had a flat end.

1-C11 EGYPTIAN — HAIRSTYLE

Due to hot climate, and a penchant for hygiene, Egyptian men kept hair closely cropped or shaved.

1-C12

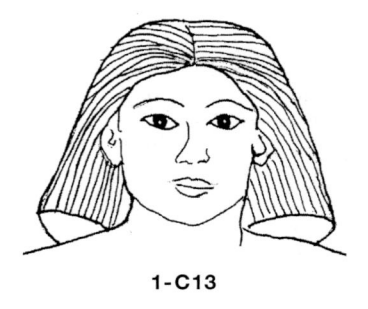

1-C13

1-C12   EGYPTIAN — SHOULDER LENGTH WIG
For formal occasions, both men and women wore wigs made from part human, part animal hair coated with wax and resin.

1-C13   EGYPTIAN — FLARED WIG
Later in the time period, wigs could be quite long and massive in proportion. The silhouette in this wig is thick and wide and exposes the ears.

1-C14   EGYPTIAN — SHEATH GOWN
The basic women's dress was tubular in shape and straight. Although illustrations show this garment as very fitted, it may be more of an illustration style. Top of skirt fell just below bust and held up by two straps that went over the bust. In this illustration, she is seen carrying offerings, possibly wine, and she is wearing a longer three-part wig.

1-C15   EGYPTIAN — SHEATH GOWN
In this illustration, the straps connect in the center below the bust, which creates a V-neck line. She is wearing a flared wig similar to the one in 1-C13.

1-C16   EGYPTIAN — PLEATED LINEN GOWN
The style of dress is similar to a kimono. It is made of a pleated sheer fabric, possibly linen, and overlaps in the front. It is held in place by a girdle, which creates the line of the sleeve. Both men and women wore this style.

1-C17   EGYPTIAN — CROWN
The royal diadem is made of gold, and precious stones. They often had motifs of flowers. There is a sacred uraeus in the center front, which indicates it was worn by a queen.

1-C18   EGYPTIAN — HATHOR HEADDRESS
This headpiece is comprised of the solar disc in the middle and flanked by cow's horns. It is a symbol of the goddess Hathor.

1-C19   EGYPTIAN — VULTURE HEADDRESS COMBINATION
This headdress is a combination of a "Double Feathers" crown, usually falcon or ostrich, which was often paired with a sun disk or ram's horns, signified by the god Amun, and the Vulture Headdress.

1-C14

1-C15

1-C16

1-C17

1-C18

1-C19

1-C20

1-C22a

1-C22b

1-C21

1-C23

1-C20   EGYPTIAN — FLARED WIG AND USEKH NECKLACE
She is wearing a heavy, shoulder length wig secured by a band.
The necklace, which is sometimes referred to as a collar, was
semi-circular in line and made of strings of beads with a row of
pendants at the base.

1-C21   EGYPTIAN — KOHL
Kohl was black eyeliner made from a mineral. It was worn by both
men and women and protected the eye from the sun.

1-C22   EGYPTIAN — CROOK AND FLAIL
The crook (22a) and flail (22b) are symbols of the King's authority
and rule. The crook is shaped like a shepherd's crook and the
flail consisted of a handle with three strands of beads. Both were
made of gold.

1-C23   EGYPTIAN — PECTORAL
The pectoral was a large decorative ornament, hanging from
a strand of beads that was worn over the chest. Designs were
based on symbols of the gods and goddesses or sacred symbols.

1-C24

1-C25

1-C26

1-C24   GREEK — LONG IONIC CHITON

The chiton is the basic garment for both males and females in ancient Greece. The rectangular fabric is wrapped around the body and attached at the shoulders and along the edges of the sleeves with fibulae. The Ionic style was worn by men and women, and emulates the line of the volutes in the Ionic capitals. The circular lines can be seen in the sleeves and the draping of the fabric.

1-C25   GREEK — SHORT IONIC CHITON

This shorter chiton was worn by younger males, and also used in conjunction with armor for the military. The garment is girdled at the waist with an overfold and additional girdling on top.

1-C26   GREEK — IONIC CHITON AND CHLAMYS

The chlamys is a short cape made from a rectangular piece of cloth that attaches on the right shoulder using a fibula.

1-C27   1-C28

1-C27   GREEK – HIMATION
Himation is a long overgarment that is rectangular in line and drapes around the body. It is sometimes worn alone or over a chiton. This is the forerunner to the toga worn by Roman men.

1-C28   GREEK – CHLAMYS
The chlamys is a short cape that attaches on one shoulder with a fibula.

1-C29   GREEK – CHLAMYS AND PETASOS
Travelers are depicted as wearing the chlamys along with a broad brimmed hat called a petasos to protect them from the sun.

1-C30   GREEK – CUIRASS, SIDE VIEW
The cuirass is a breastplate made of leather or cast bronze that is worn by soldiers. It has a skirt of leather tabs that is attached to the waistline of the breastplate. It is usually worn over a short Ionic chiton.

1-C31   GREEK – CUIRASS, HELMET AND GREAVES
This illustration shows the front view of the cuirass with the shoulder pieces. It is decorated on the front chest area. See images 1-C32 and 1-C33 for details on helmet and greaves.

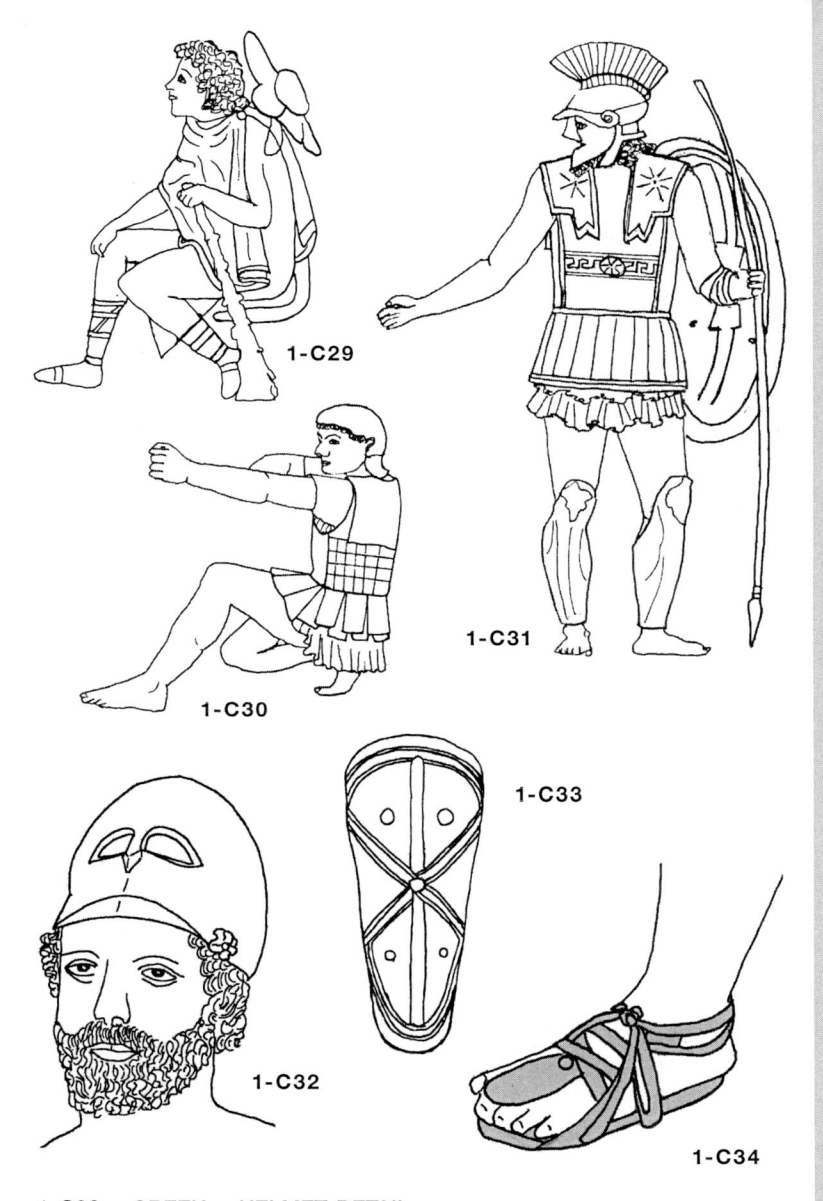

1-C29

1-C31

1-C30

1-C33

1-C32

1-C34

1-C32   GREEK — HELMET DETAIL
The helmet in this image is made of metal with a crest of horsehair or feathers and covers the face with holes for eyes and nose.

1-C33   GREEK — GREAVES
Greaves are shin guards worn by the military. They are often made of metal.

1-C34   GREEK — SANDAL
This is a closeup of a sandal that shows the intricate use of straps to attach the sandal to the foot. The sandals are made of leather.

1-C35

1-C36

1-C35   GREEK — FILLET
The fillet is a hairband made of leather and decorated with symbols such as the chi. It tied in the back of the head with a strap.

1-C36   GREEK — MALE HAIRSTYLE
Short and curly hair was popular with men. They were often clean-shaven but we also see evidence of beards as in 1-C32.

1-C37   GREEK — DORIC CHITON
This style of chiton was worn by women only, and resembles the Doric column. It is composed of two rectangles of cloth (often wool) that are folded over, secured at the shoulder using fibulae, and girdled at the waist. Much like the Doric column, it has an overall horizontal line.

1-C38   GREEK — IONIC CHITON AND HIMATION
The Ionic chiton for women was consistent with the style worn by men. The women often have an overfold that extends to the lower calf. The himation is wrapped in much the same way as the men.

1-C39   GREEK — IONIC CHITON AND HIMATION
In this illustration, the overfold is folded back under and attached at the waist creating a bit more fullness in the body of the chiton.

1-C40   GREEK — DORIC CHITON
This side view illustrates the line and draping of the sleeve and overfold on the Doric chiton.

1-C41   GREEK — IONIC CHITON
The sleeve details can clearly be seen in this side view closeup of the Ionic chiton. The sleeves are attached by using fibulae to pin the edges together at regular intervals. This arrangement creates the circular volute-like silhouette.

1-C37

1-C38

1-C39

1-C40

1-C41

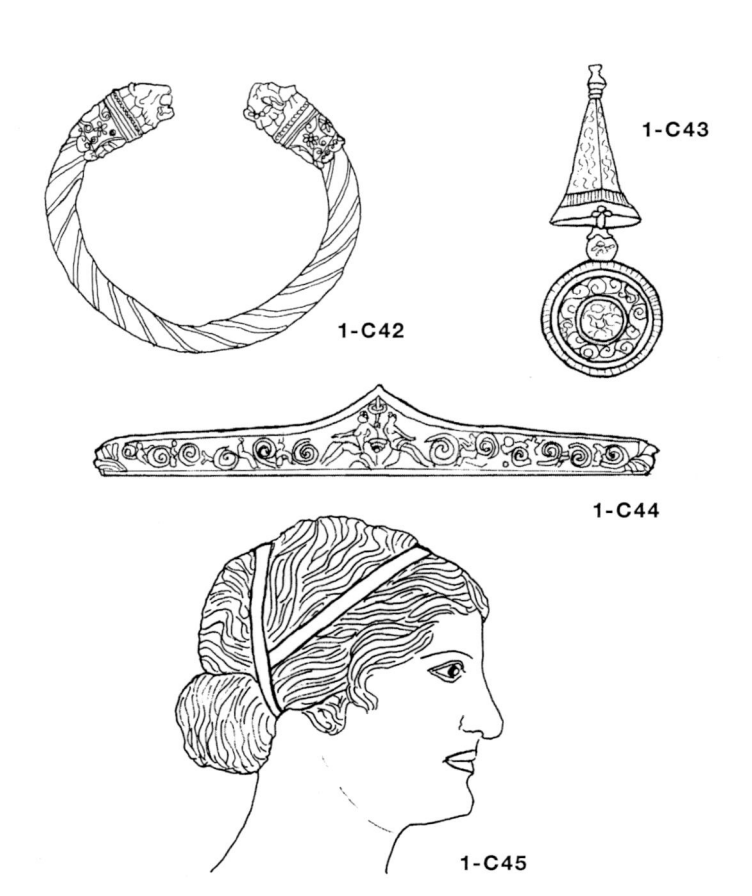

1-C42

1-C43

1-C44

1-C45

1-C42   GREEK — BRACELET

The most common type of bracelet is a large hoop of gold, with an animal head on each end. Common animal motifs included lions, bulls, and rams. Bracelets could be worn on both the lower as well as upper arms, and often worn in pairs.

1-C43   GREEK — EARRING

The pendant style of earrings, in gold or silver, was the most popular. These were often worn with matching bracelets and necklaces.

1-C44   GREEK — DIADEM

A diadem is similar to a tiara or half-crown. This particular one has embossed designs composed of several figures (Dionysus and Ariadne) with additional arabesques.

1-C45   GREEK — HAIRSTYLE

The women's hairstyles were relaxed and featured curls framing the face with hair pulled up into a simple chignon and ribbons laced through the hair.

1-C46

1-C48

1-C47

1-C46 & 1-C47   ROMAN — LONG TUNIC AND TOGA

Basic male garment (tunica) is rectangular in silhouette and similar to the Greek chiton. It is generally made up of two rectangles that were sewn at the shoulder line and along the sides with openings for the neck and arms. In later periods, sleeves were added. It is girdled at the waist. The outer garment known as the toga, is semi-circular in shape, and was worn by male citizens. It often had a border on the center (straight) edge of the garment. The color of the toga and border indicated the rank in society. This could be worn as a head covering on certain occasions.

1-C48   ROMAN — SHORT TUNIC

The shorter version of the tunic, also girdled at the waist, was worn by younger males or in conjunction with the breastplate for those in the military.

1-C49

1-C50

1-C51

1-C49   ROMAN — BREASTPLATE

A common style of breastplate for ordinary infantrymen is made of plaited leather with metal fittings. It is worn over a pleated short tunic.

1-C50   ROMAN — BREASTPLATE (CUIRASS)

The breastplate or cuirass, worn by the military, could be made of bronze, iron, or leather. It often was embellished with reliefs that depicted battles, gods, and other symbols of Roman power. This illustration represents a bronze or iron breastplate that conforms to the musculature of the body underneath. The rigid metal breastplate was cumbersome on the battlefield, and more commonly worn by emperors in ceremonial occasions.

1-C51   ROMAN — HELMET

Roman helmets varied in style. This is an example of a metal helmet with a crest on top. The crest was made of either plumes or horsehair, and generally worn by commanders or higher ranking officers. The helmet has ear and neck guards as well as embossed "eyebrows" or shield. Some had nose or cheek guards as well. Earlier helmets were made of leather.

1-C52

1-C53

1-C54

1-C55

1-C52   ROMAN — HAIRSTYLE

Men often devoted time to dressing the hair, while using curling devices to achieve the curled look, which was popular. Beards and mustaches were common in the early part of the Empire.

1-C53   ROMAN — LAUREL WREATH HEADDRESS

In ancient Rome, these were made from the leaves of the laurel tree and shaped like a horseshoe. It symbolized victory or power. Emperors and victorious commanders were often depicted wearing these.

1-C54 & 1-C55   ROMAN — STOLA AND PALLA

The basic garment worn by women was similar to the Greek style chiton and known as a stola or tunic. It was fashioned from two rectangular pieces of fabric seamed at the shoulders and sides with openings for the arms and neck. A belt (girdle) was worn at the waist. Later in the time period, the stola could have sleeves as seen in 1-C55. The palla is similar to the Greek himation and could be worn pulled up over the head or draped around the stola.

41

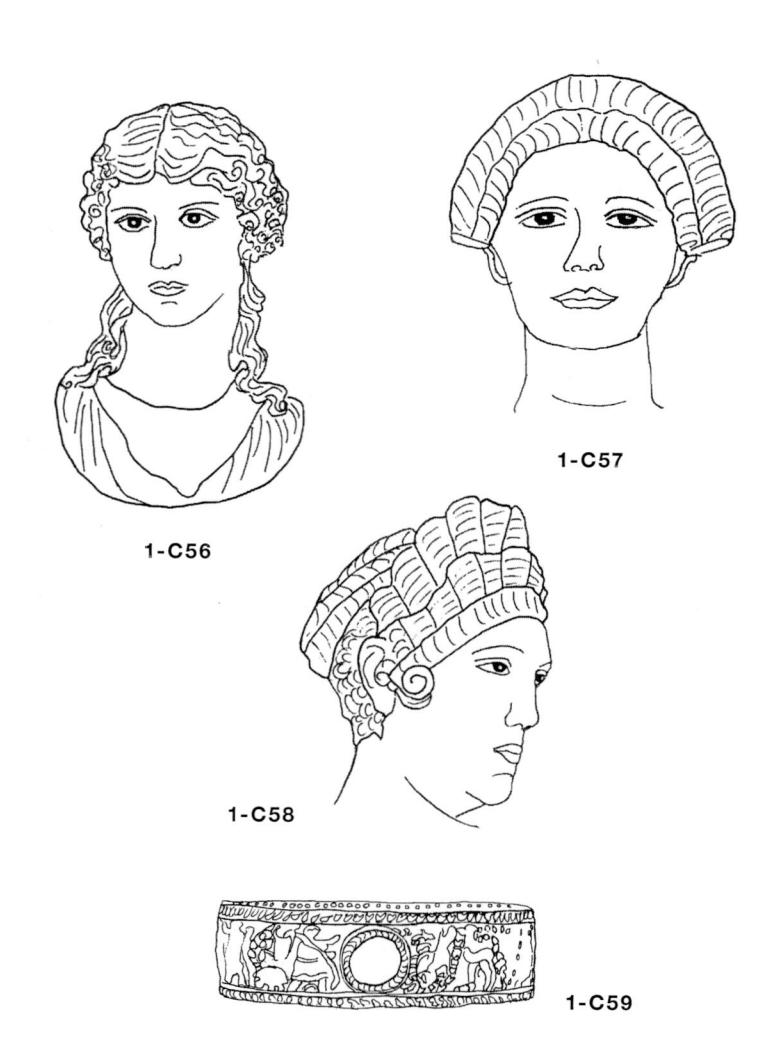

1-C57

1-C56

1-C58

1-C59

1-C56 ROMAN — HAIRSTYLE

The earlier, simplified style was similar to the soft curled hairstyles of the Greek women. This relaxed natural style gives way to the more structured and formal style in the later period. See 1-C57 and 1-C58.

1-C57 & 1-C58 ROMAN — HAIRSTYLES

Styling of the hair was given much attention by women during the later Roman period. It often required the services of a hairdresser who would use a combination of hair and wigs to create the structures that surround the face.

1-C59 ROMAN — BRACELET

Bracelets were often engraved with symbolic images and figured scenes. Gold was the predominant material.

Medieval Period

The Medieval period consists of three sections: Early Christian/Byzantine, Romanesque or Middle Ages, and Gothic. Early Christian period loosely covers a time period from 330* to 800 and Byzantine 330 to 1453. In this early period, the Roman Empire was divided between Rome, the center of the Western Roman Empire, and Constantinople, the center of the Eastern Roman Empire. Because the Eastern Byzantine Empire was located at the crossroads of the trade routes, it became rich and stable. The Western Empire did not fare as well, falling to the northern cultures in 476. The Byzantine Empire maintained until 1453 when the Ottoman Empire took control.

The Romanesque or Middle Ages period, 800 to 1100, marks the beginning of feudalism, in which communities of peasants relied on feudal lords to protect them, and the reign of Charlemagne. Castles were constructed to protect communities that were at war with each other.

The Gothic period, 1100 to 1400, begins to reflect a social stability that brings about development of trade, manufacturing, and finance. These advances enabled centers of religion and commerce to develop. These centers in turn created great cathedrals, developed sophisticated weaving industries and tailoring techniques, and introduced silk from the East.

Architecture/Furniture/Décor

Each of these periods reflects a distinct stylistic influence. The Early Christian/Byzantine period is influenced by the style of the existing Roman temples that were converted into Christian churches, combined with the Middle Eastern style resulting from trade with the East. This combination of cultures was seen in the stylized capitals and columns, as well as in the use of mosaics to communicate Christian symbols. Romanesque would take the architectural elements of the traditional Roman structures and repurpose them to church construction, adding elements that gave the churches a defensive look. Gothic would attempt to create an environment of

---

*All dates are CE unless otherwise noted.

verticality that would visually lift the viewer's eyes toward the heavens and incorporate local images from various cultures that may not have been Christian in origin. Furniture, although also influenced in the same way as architecture, would at first divorce itself from its Classical beginnings, but eventually catch up to the level of craftsmanship that the Classical period had achieved.

Costume

During the Byzantine period, mosaics and statues provide much of the information we have for clothing, and almost all images are of royalty or religious icons. Clothing styles evolved from Roman dress with additional elements reflecting the more ornamental dress of the Eastern countries. In the early Middle Ages, much of the figurative art was destroyed during the wars because it was deemed sacrilegious. What remains depicts government, military, and church figures, most of which are male. Styles do not change significantly except for a reduction in ornamentation. Toward the latter end of this period, illuminated manuscripts become a reliable source of clothing styles. Silk is introduced into Europe and trade guilds specializing in textiles begin. Research for the Gothic period includes illuminated manuscripts, tomb effigies, and tapestries, and at the very end of the period, paintings. Cloth guilds expand, patternmaking and fitting skills are more advanced, and tailors existed for both men and women. Fabric choices included silk, brocades, satin, and velvet.

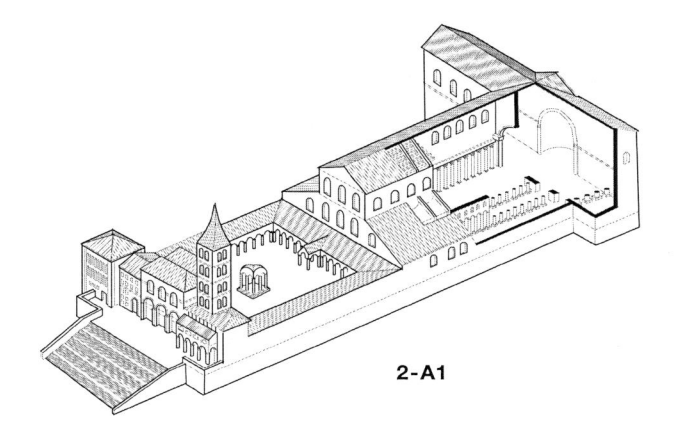

2-A1

2-A2

2-A1 EARLY CHRISTIAN BASILICA OF ST. PETER
Based on a Latin cross ground plan, with an atrium and well or fountain in the atrium. Rome, Italy. 350.

2-A2 EARLY CHRISTIAN BASILICA OF ST. PETER SECTION VIEW
The nave of early St. Peter's Basilica contained two side aisles, with columns supporting the upper walls that were taken from Roman temples. Beams in the ceiling were open.

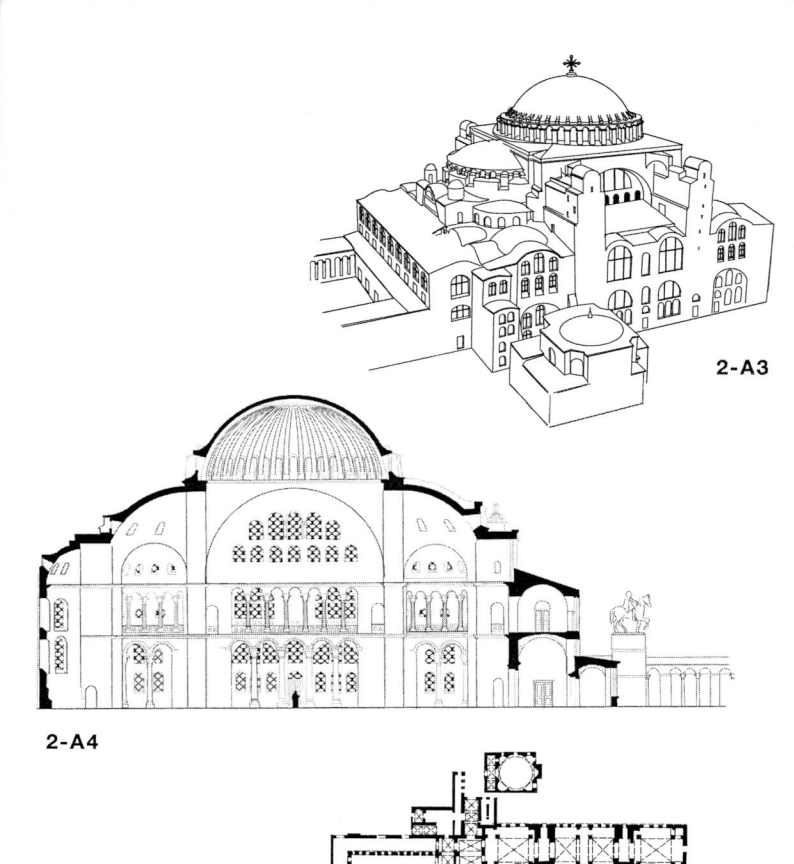

2-A3

2-A4

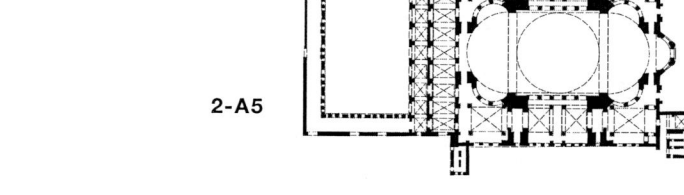

2-A5

2-A3 HAGIA SOPHIA

A Byzantine church, Hagia Sophia in Constantinople is based on the Greek cross format. Construction techniques established in the Roman Empire have been incorporated into this structure such as the dome, arches, and vaults, and the use of mosaics on the interior. 537.

2-A4 HAGIA SOPHIA SECTION

The dome is 102 feet across and 180 feet off of the floor. This large dome sits on two arches which transfer the load to the four main piers. This allows the space to be opened up more than typical church structures.

2-A5 HAGIA SOPHIA GROUND PLAN

The ground plan of Hagia Sophia is based on the Greek cross format. Like many of the Early Christian churches, this structure also had an atrium connected to the main entrance of the structure.

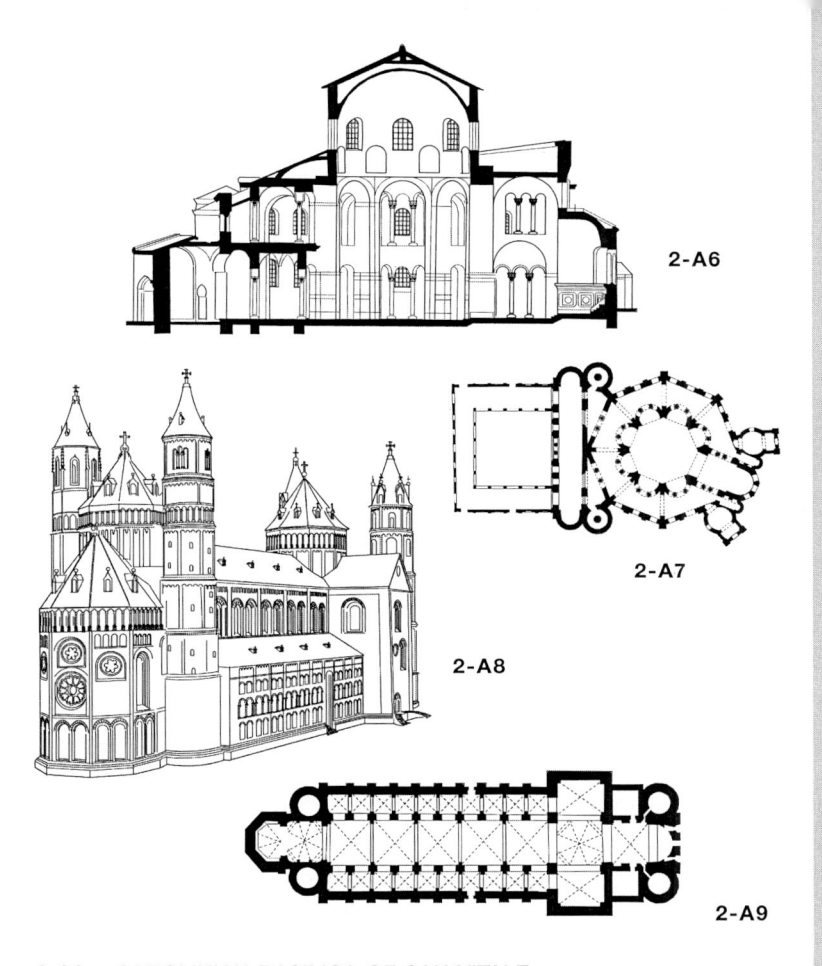

2-A6

2-A7

2-A8

2-A9

2-A6   CAROLINIAN BASILICA OF SAN VITALE
Located in Ravenna, Italy, San Vitale is a smaller structure similar to Hagia Sophia, with a Latin cross format and an ambulatory around the center. 547.

2-A7   CAROLINIAN BASILICA OF SAN VITALE GROUND PLAN
Using the Latin cross, the ground plan is based on an octagonal plan with eight piers and an atrium on one end.

2-A8   ST. PETER'S DOM (WORMSER DOM)
This church, located in Worms, Germany, is in the Romanesque style, based on a Latin cross format. Round arched windows, vaults, and a heavier look are part of this style's characteristics. 1181.

2-A9   ST. PETER'S DOM GROUND PLAN
The Worms Cathedral has a long nave with four towers. The transept is located near the entrance, and has two domes and two choirs, one on either end. The Cathedral ground plan is based on a Latin cross, except that the transept is closer to the entrance than the apse.

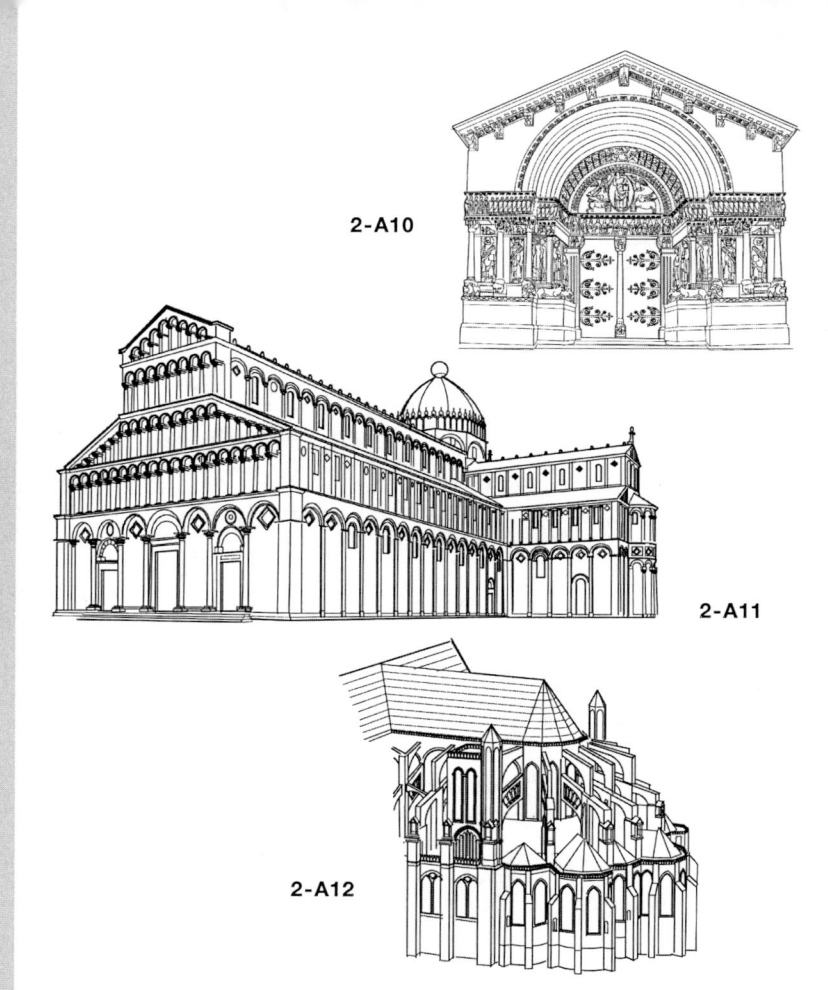

2-A10

2-A11

2-A12

2-A10   ROMANESQUE PORTAL OF ST. TROPHIME
The Romanesque portal, or entrance of the church, has the image of the Apocalypse carved above the entrance with the Apostles below. It is located in Arles, France. 1190.

2-A11   DUOMO DI SANTA MARIA ASSUNTA
The cathedral in Pisa in the Tuscany region of Italy, is considered the best example of Italian Romanesque style. The main entrance has rows of arched columns from just above the portal to the top of the portico. Multicolored marble is used on the exterior, unlike the Romanesque style found in other countries. 1064.

2-A12   CHARTRES CATHEDRAL
Located in France, Chartres Cathedral is in the Gothic style based on a Latin cross format. The flying buttress is a significant element of the Gothic style. The purpose is to transfer the weight of the ceiling from the walls of the nave past the side aisles to the outside piers. This enables the walls of the nave to have larger windows placed into them. 1250.

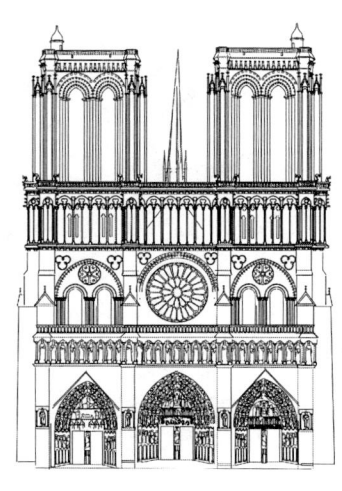

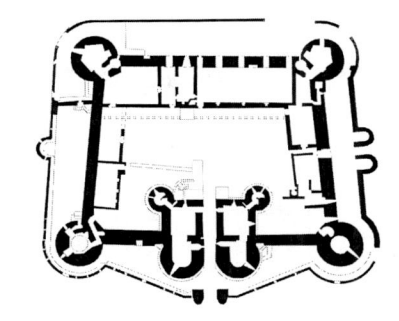

2-A13

2-A14

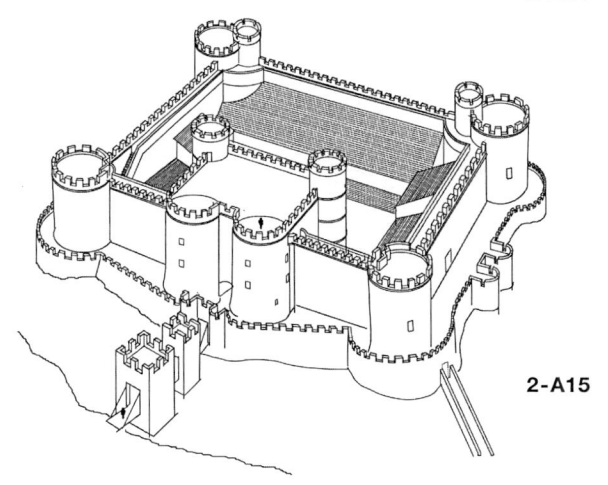

2-A15

2-A13   PORTALS AND FAÇADE OF THE CATHEDRAL NOTRE DAME
The façade of Notre Dame in Paris, France, is considered a
traditional Gothic style. Three portals with sculpted figures
establish the main entrance into the church. A rose window
is located in the center with a screen of columns above. This
is capped with twin bell towers. The effect is to draw the eye
upward. 1245.

2-A14   HARLECH CASTLE GROUND PLAN
Illustrated here are the inner and outer wards, or walls, for
protection. The keep doubles as the gatehouse, as well.

2-A15   HARLECH CASTLE
Located on the coast of Wales, Harlech Castle is considered
typical of castle structures of its time. An inner ward or wall is
pictured with a ditch for protection. Two ditch towers and a bridge
were also in the original structure. 1289.

2-A16

2-A17

2-A18

2-A19

2-A16 JACQUES COEUR PALACE

Jacques Coeur, who became the treasurer to King Charles VII of France, built this rambling structure around a courtyard. The palace is located in Bourges, France. 1451.

2-A17 JACQUES COEUR PALACE GROUND PLAN

This ground plan illustrates a structure that is built around a courtyard. The main entrance is on the lower right of the courtyard area.

2-A18 MERCHANT'S HOUSE

Located in Southampton, England, this illustrates the half-timber construction technique with planked doors and stave grills used in place of glass windows. 1290.

2-A19 PALAZZO VECCHIO

This structure was built in the early 14th century as a palace and government building in Florence, Italy. It has high trefoil arch windows. The tower is off-center, taking advantage of an already existing foundation (from a previous structure).

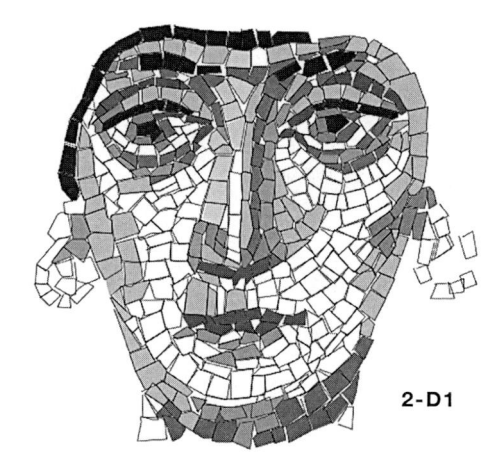

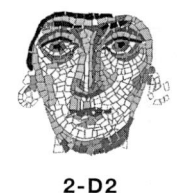

2-D2

2-D1

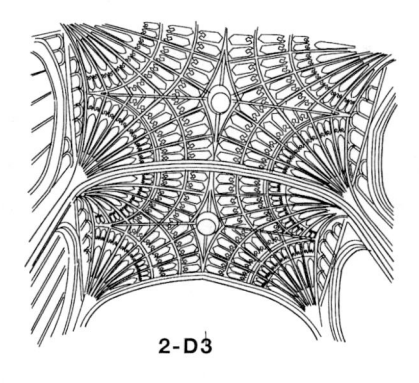

2-D3

2-D4

2-D1 MOSAIC OF EMPRESS THEODORA
This mosaic is made with gold, jewels, small stones, metal, and glass placed in wet plaster. The mosaic is found in San Vitale. 547.

2-D2 VIEW OF MOSAIC FROM A DISTANCE
Although appearing crude up close, the long view from those in the church would cause the stones to blend together. Some stones and glass would be set on a slight angle, causing the image to glitter.

2-D3 KING'S COLLEGE CHAPEL FAN VAULT
The fan vault of King's College Chapel, located in Cambridge, England, is in the late Gothic style. 1515.

2-D4 DURHAM CATHEDRAL
The interior of this Romanesque church located in Durham, England has round arches with thick columns, many of which have geometric designs. 1018.

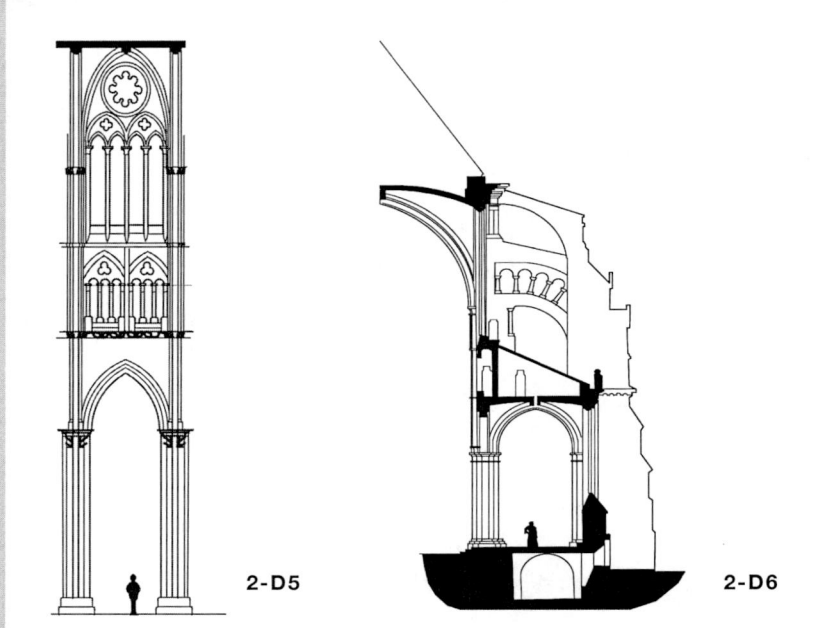

2-D5

2-D6

2-D5 CHARTRES CATHEDRAL GOTHIC WALL DETAILS
Illustrated on the Chartres Cathedral nave walls are clustered columns, a tall Gothic arch, and elongated clerestory Gothic windows, all visually giving the appearance of height and open wall space. 1220.

2-D6 CHARTRES CATHEDRAL SECTION
Chartres Cathedral used buttressing (as illustrated) to transfer the load of the ceiling away from the nave walls, allowing larger window spaces to be created. 1220.

2-D7 GOTHIC ARCH
The Gothic arch is a pointed arch that helps distribute the ceiling load to the outside walls.

2-D8 CINQUEFOIL ARCH
This consists of a tracery or inset with five pendants located in a Gothic arch.

2-D9 OGEE ARCH
This arch consists of two S curves that create a pointed arch for use as decoration, not structure.

2-D10 TUDOR ARCH
This arch is a low-profile arch which, although it possesses a subtle point, is very muted when compared to the Gothic.

2-D11 TIE BEAM ARCH
Located in the Great Malvern Hall in Worcester, England, this uses decorative bracing to create stability and load transfer. A connecting beam between the supports gives this structure its name. 1340.

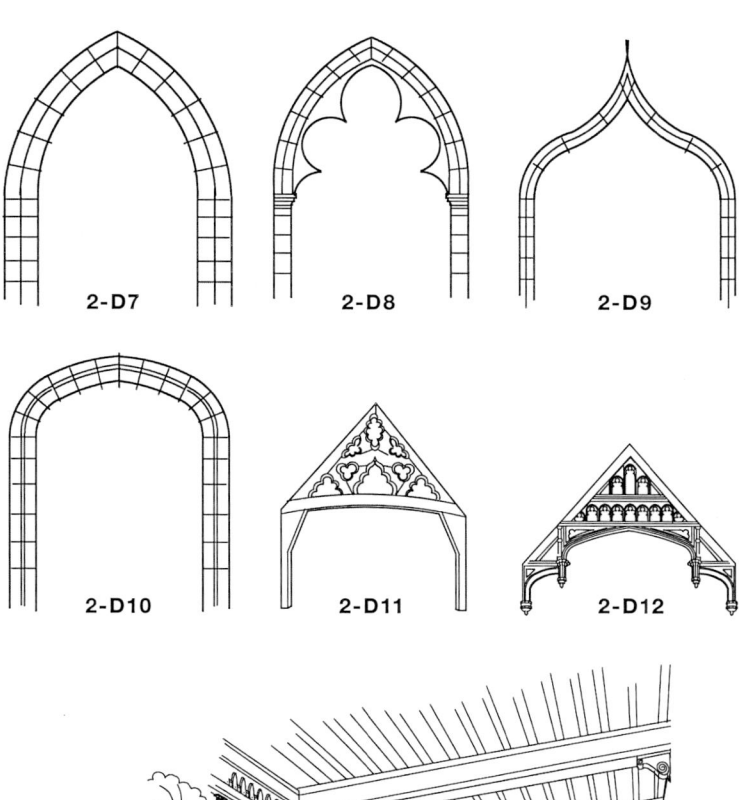

2-D7

2-D8

2-D9

2-D10

2-D11

2-D12

2-D13

2-D12   HAMMER BEAM ARCH

Located in the Great Hall of Eltham Palace in London, this arch illustrates a tiered effect in the transferring of load, creating stability in a decorative way.

2-D13   PALAZZO DAVANZATI

The Parrot Room of the Palazzo Davanzati is so named because of the parrot images incorporated into the wall paintings of drapery. Windows have bifold shutters, painted beams, and a frieze painting depicting the life of the Lady of Vergi. 14th century.

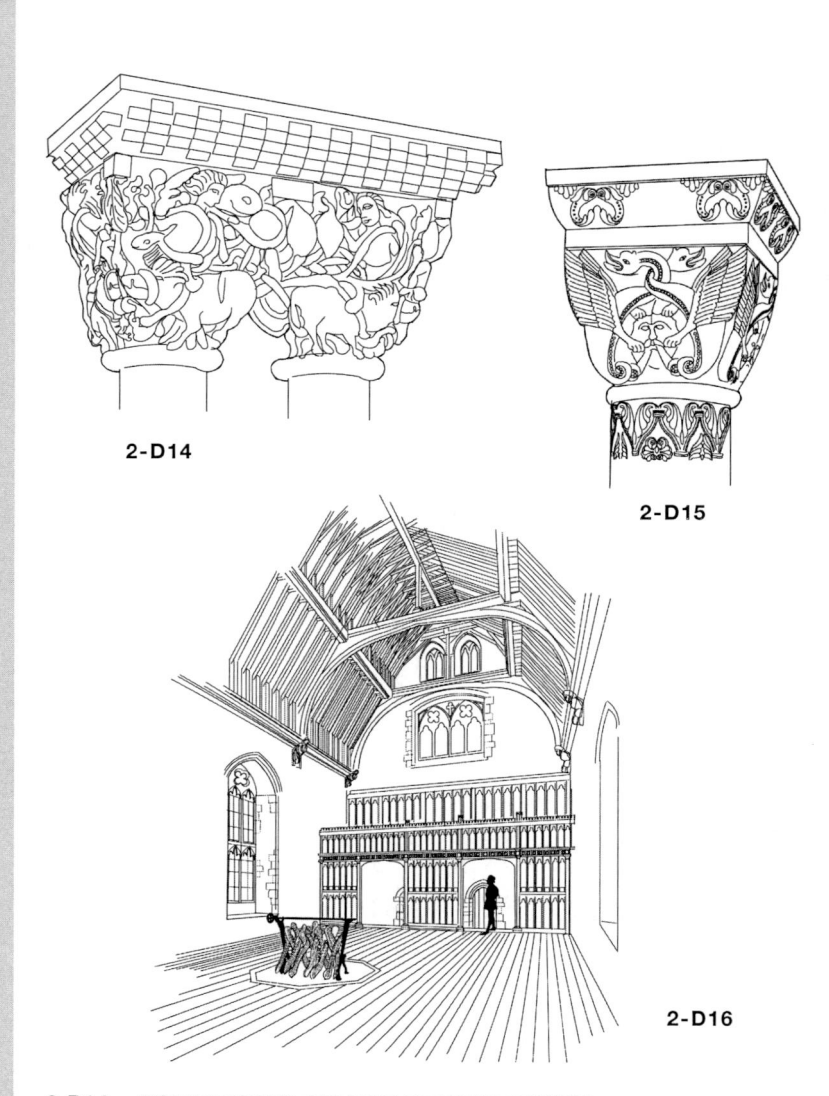

2-D14

2-D15

2-D16

2-D14   ROMANESQUE DOUBLE COLUMN CAPITAL
This capital illustrates how the double column capital can be used to create a single support. 12th century.

2-D15   MEDIEVAL CAPITAL
This capital combines Classical acanthus leaves with winged dragons and human figures. 1167–1200.

2-D16   THE GREAT HALL AT PENHURST
The Great Hall at Penhurst, England, illustrates most of the elements incorporated into great halls of this time, which include large windows, a fire pit, and wood paneling or a screen at one end of the room. Two doors allowed access to the hallway that included a door to the pantry and another to the butlery. 1341.

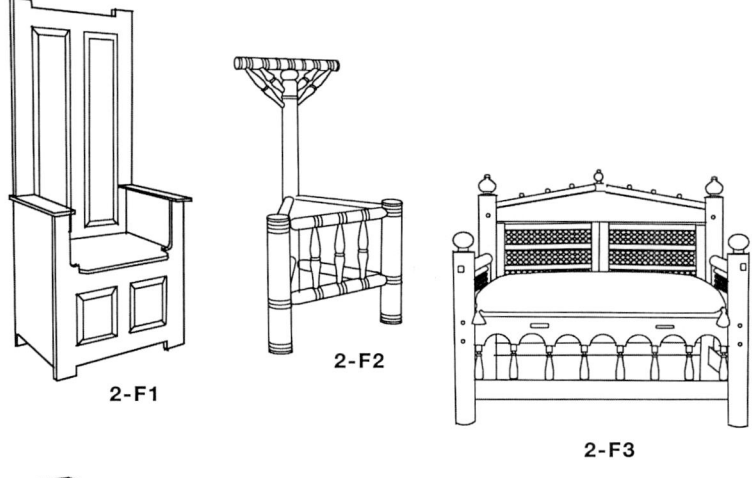

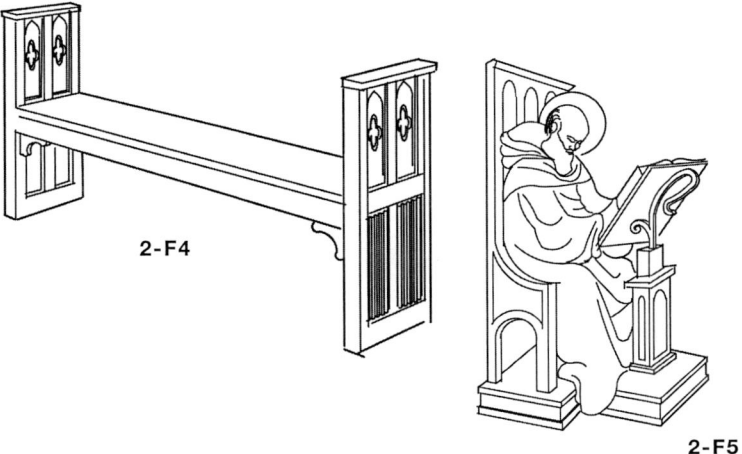

2-F1   MEDIEVAL BOX CHAIR
Box chairs, like the name, were built around a box which made up the seat. A back and arms were added.

2-F2   THREE-LEGGED STOOL WITH A BACK
The simplicity of this piece of furniture made it a popular design.

2-F3   BISHOP'S CHAIR WITH PILLOW
This is a Byzantine-style chair with wood spindle supports. 12th century.

2-F4   BROAD BENCH
This broad bench has a Gothic design on the armrests, and linenfold patterns on the lower portion.

2-F5   CHAIR AND LECTERN
The illustration of St. Jerome in his study with chair and lectern was a popular combination at this time.

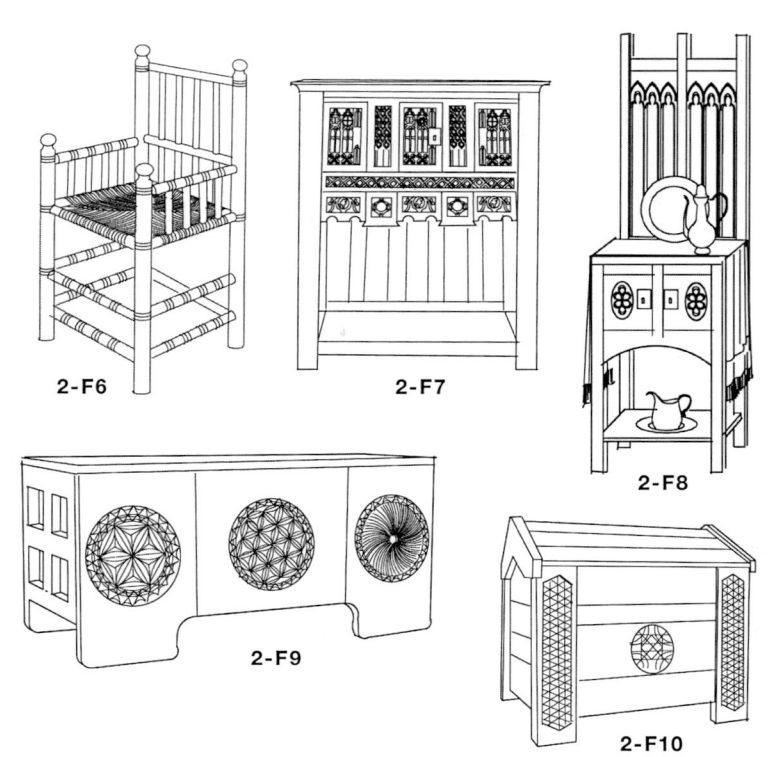

2-F6

2-F7

2-F8

2-F9

2-F10

2-F6   MEDIEVAL ARM CHAIR

Much like the box chair, this design is based on a box structure
made of spindle supports with a woven rush seat.

2-F7   MEDIEVAL CREDENCE CUPBOARD

Used for dining and preparation of food much like a sideboard,
these pieces of furniture would incorporate Gothic style and
linenfold patterns in their decoration. The lower half was used for
display of plateware.

2-F8   DRESSOIR CUPBOARD

A dressoir cupboard is very similar to the buffet. The name refers
to the dressing boards which were used to dress the meal. It
typically contained food and plateware and many times had a
cloth draped over it.

2-F9   MEDIEVAL CHEST

Chests at this time were fairly simple units with a hinged lid and a
locking device. Decorations could be carved into the surface, as
indicated on this chest. Late 13th century.

2-F10   MEDIEVAL GABLED CHEST

A chest of this type would have had a lid that was either gabled or
curved to protect the contents from the elements.

2-F11   THREE-LEGGED STOOL

This stool with spindle supports would have had a woven reed or
leather seat. It worked well when placed on uneven ground.

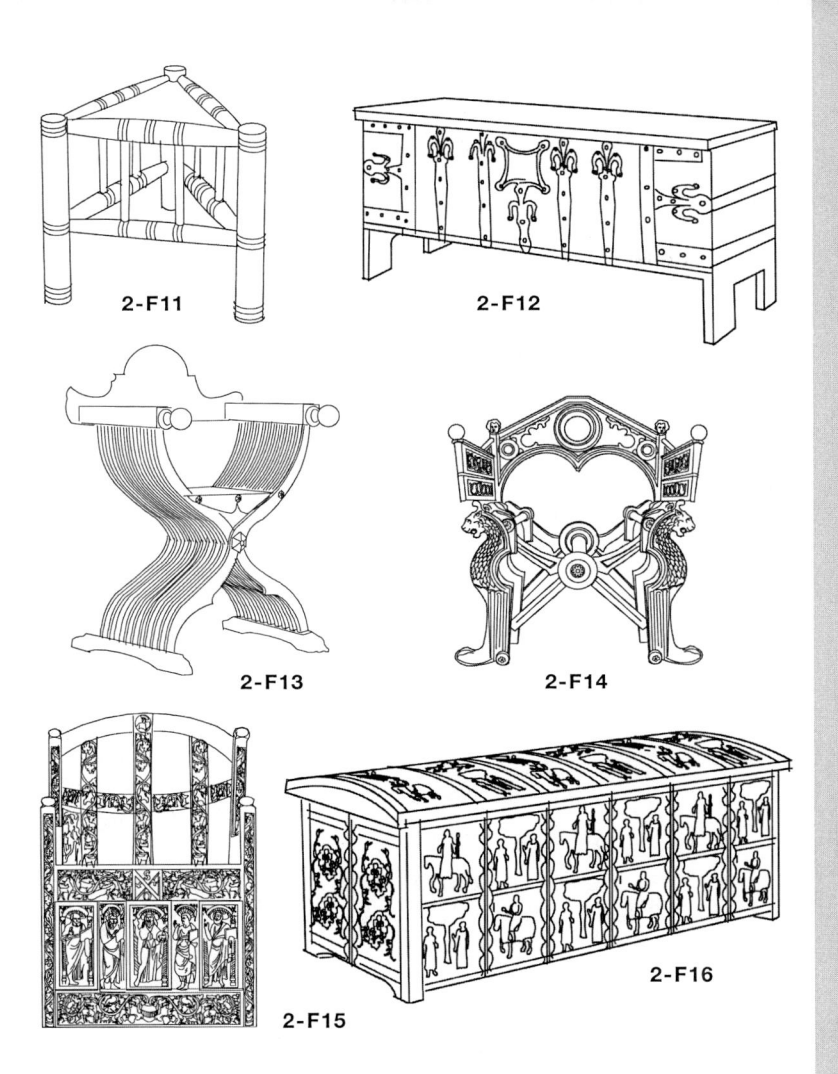

2-F11

2-F12

2-F13

2-F14

2-F15

2-F16

2-F12 MEDIEVAL GERMAN CHEST
Located in Castle Coburg, Germany, this chest uses iron strapping as both support and decoration. 13th century.

2-F13 MEDIEVAL SAVONAROLA OR DONTIE FOLDING CHAIR
This chair, sometimes called the X chair, is based on a chair that would fold, but over time became too elaborate for this purpose.

2-F14 THRONE OF DAGOBERT
Attributed to Dagobert the Merovingian King, it has the lion's leg and head with a back and arms. 639.

2-F15 THRONE OF MAXIMIAN
This Byzantine throne has panels of carved ivory depicting religious scenes and saints. 553.

2-F16 MEDIEVAL WEDDING CHEST
This Italian wedding chest has painted scenes of love. 1354.

2-C1

2-C2

2-C3

2-C1   MID 6TH CENTURY

The tunic is similar to the style in the Roman Period, which had long fitted sleeves and is girdled at the waist. The length could be below knee or to the ankle. There is a rondel on the shoulder of the tunic, which is a round applique decoration. The palludamentum, which is the cape attached on one shoulder using a fibula or brooch, was worn by upper class men including the Emperor depicted here, and the Empress.

2-C2   MID 6TH CENTURY

The clerical vestments that were worn at this time are the basis for the modern vestments still used in many of the Christian religions. The alb is the long white undertunic with narrow sleeves, the overgarment with shorter and wider sleeves is known as a chasuable, and sometimes referred to as a dalmatica in non-clerical garments. The stole is the narrow strip that is worn over the shoulders and often has a cross.

2-C3   MID 7TH CENTURY

The male in this image is wearing a long tunic and a palludamentum with a tablion, which is a large square applique traditionally positioned over the chest near the front edge.

2-C4

2-C5

2-C6

2-C4   LATE 8TH CENTURY

This male is wearing an undertunic, which has a wide collar, known as a cowl, worn over the neckline of the tunic. The tunic is wider in both the body and the sleeves than previous and the girdling is below the waist.

2-C5   LATE 8TH CENTURY

This male, presumably a monk, is wearing a sleeveless garment over his undertunic with a cowl collar, and a cape over his shoulders. Monks would traditionally shave the top of their head, with a fringe of hair from ear to ear.

2-C6   LATE 8TH CENTURY

The King is wearing an undertunic with fitted sleeves and a cowl, along with a hood. This gives you a side view of the hood. The hood is a forerunner to the academic regalia hood that is worn today.

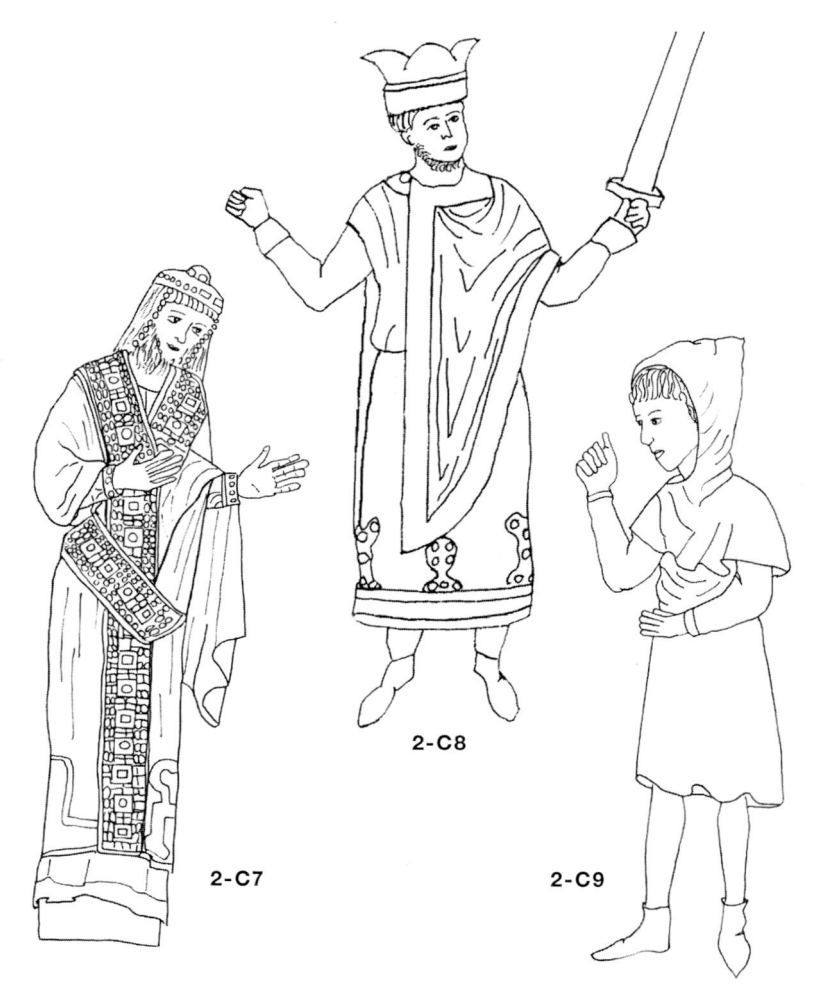

2-C8

2-C7

2-C9

2-C7 MID 10TH CENTURY

We continue to see the Byzantine look late into the Middle Ages in certain areas of the Eastern countries. The headdress is elaborate and very beaded, along with the lorum which is the heavily jeweled scarf worn over the tunic.

2-C8 EARLY 11TH CENTURY

The tunics become shorter in length and worn above the ankle. The embroidery at the bottom edge of the garment is common with men of nobility and rank, in this case a King. The cape is also shorter and semi-circular in shape. The boots during this time period were often ankle length and made of leather or cloth.

2-C9 MID 12TH CENTURY

This shepherd is wearing a knee-length tunic girdled at the waist, and soft boots. The hood and chaperon (cape) is worn over the tunic. As the tunics became shorter, the legs were covered with braies, a two-piece knitted hose that was belted at the waist.

2-C11

2-C10

2-C10   MID 13TH CENTURY

The outer tunic has hanging sleeves that end at the elbows with long extensions called tippets. He is also wearing the hood and chaperon, and striped braies.

2-C11   MID 13TH CENTURY

The male in this image is wearing a knee-length undertunic, over which is worn a shorter tunic with dagging (scalloped edge) on the hem and sleeves. The hat has two pieces: a coif or cap underneath that ties at the neck, and a short brim soft hat worn over the coif.

2-C12   MID 13TH CENTURY

The sleeveless over garment with the large armholes, known as a surcote, is worn over a long undertunic and a hood.

2-C12

2-C14

2-C13

2-C15

2-C13   EARLY 15TH CENTURY

This image shows a side view of a decorated knee-length tunic, with short sleeves that end at the elbow, worn over an undertunic with fitted sleeves. Boots have a cuff and are calf-length.

2-C14   MID 15TH CENTURY

The houppelande worn by this male is a sleeveless outer garment that is calf-length and generally pleated, giving it a fairly wide silhouette. The edge of the garments could be trimmed in fur. The wide hat was common in the Netherlands.

2-C15   LATE 9TH CENTURY

Military garment consisting of a tunic, short cape (palludamentum), which was often blue, and fastened with a brooch. The hose in this image is secured above the knee with garters and the boots are calf-length. A small purse is tied onto the belt.

2-C16

2-C17

2-C18

2-C16 EARLY 11TH CENTURY

Military garment consisting of a tunic, an outer layer that consists of a breastplate, usually made of metal or leather and a skirt consisting of rows of leather tabs which can also be found on the sleeves. He also has a mantle (cape) and calf-length boots.

2-C17 13TH CENTURY

Side view of a military garment that consists of the undertunic, breastplate to below the waist, skirt and sleeve with tabs, and long mantle.

2-C18 15TH CENTURY

The tunic in this military garment has a geometric pattern, which is carried through in the mantle. The boots with straps are calf-length.

2-C19

2-C20

2-C21

2-C22

2-C23

2-C24

2-C19 & 2-C20   10TH CENTURY

These two images illustrate two silhouettes that were common for helmets used by the military.

2-C21   MID 13TH CENTURY

This hat, with a large brim and low crown, is an example of one that would be worn by a traveler or worker.

2-C22   MID 15TH CENTURY

The turban was a popular style later in the period. They were made of fabric and wrapped around the head and tied.

2-C23   MID 15TH CENTURY

This wide soft hat has a tail, which is referred to as a liripipe. The tails had a pointed end and could be several feet long.

2-C24   MID 15TH CENTURY

The sugar loaf hat was made of wool and resembled a loaf of bread.

2-C26

2-C25   2-C27

2-C25 EARLY 5TH CENTURY

The garments reflect the full regalia of an Empress in the Byzantine era. The basic garment is called a stola, as it was in the Roman era. The stola has trim encrusted with jewels and was cinched at the waist with a girdle. There are rondels on both sleeves as well as the lower edge of the stola. The drapery over the hips is known as the thorakion shield, and reflected the same geometric designs found on the stola.

2-C26 MID 6TH CENTURY

The Empress is wearing a palludamentum, the long rectangular cape that fastened on the shoulder with a brooch. The Empress is the only female who was allowed to wear this style. She wears a collar and crown of jewels. The crown is heavily jeweled with strings of pearls that hang from the crown.

2-C27 MID 6TH CENTURY

This woman was part of the court of the Empress and is wearing a stola with segmentum, which are square embroidered appliques as seen on the lower skirt. There is an embroidered geometric border that contains jewels. She wears a padded roll hat.

2-C28

2-C30

2-C29

2-C28   MID 13TH CENTURY

The habits of Catholic nuns in the 20th century evolved from the style of women's garments during this time period. The tunic with fitted sleeves is girdled at the waist. A band of fabric, called a gorget, wraps around the neck, and a wimple drapes around the throat and is pinned at top of head. The mantle or long cape could be worn over the head for ceremonial occasions.

2-C29   EARLY 14TH CENTURY

The woman is wearing a bliaut, which is fitted in the torso and fuller in the skirt. The sleeves are moderately wide in this example, but could extend to the bottom edge of the skirt. The skirt of the gown is open on the side revealing the fitted tunic underneath.

2-C30   MID 14TH CENTURY

The woman is wearing a sideless gown over the tunic, which is fitted to the hip. The sideless gown had wide armholes that extended to the hip line and were sometimes trimmed in fur. Over time the front panel became thinner and the armholes deeper.

2-C32

2-C31

2-C33

2-C31 LATE 14TH CENTURY
This image shows the side view of a sideless gown. The headpiece includes a barbette which is a chin band attached to her crown, and a crespinette over the hair.

2-C32 LATE 14TH CENTURY
The bliaut in this example has sleeves that are more fitted at the upper sleeve and wide at the wrist. She wears a padded roll hat.

2-C33 MID 15TH CENTURY
This is an example of a female houppelande. The neckline is high and the sleeves are very large and shaped like a large bag with a wide opening that can be trimmed in fur.

2-C34

2-C35

2-C36

2-C37

2-C34   LATE 6TH CENTURY
Example of a necklace with a Byzantine cross and pendants.

2-C35   EARLY 7TH CENTURY
Example of a crown, made of gold, that is encrusted with precious stones.

2-C36   MID 13TH CENTURY
Closeup view of the barbette and wimple. The barbette is the chin band, which attaches to the crown, and the wimple is the cloth that wraps around the neck and is attached at the top of the head. This style influenced the habit of the Catholic nuns in the 20th century.

2-C37   MID 13TH CENTURY
Closeup view of the gorget and veil. The gorget is a piece of fabric that wraps around the neck.

2-C38   MID 15TH CENTURY
This woman is wearing a veil of sheer fabric over a head covering exposing the high forehead that was popular with women during this time.

2-C38

2-C39

2-C40

2-C42

2-C41

2-C39   MID 15TH CENTURY

This is an example of a reticulated headdress, which comes to two points as if they were horns on either side of the head. This particular headdress is finished with a sheer fabric overlay.

2-C40   MID 15TH CENTURY

An example of the crespinette combined with a crown. The crespinette is netting that covered the hair. It appears her hair is styled in the popular Ramshorn headdress, which consisted of two braids over the ears.

2-C41   MID 15TH CENTURY

The headdress is known as a henin and continues to be popular through the Early Renaissance. The hat has a tall pointed conical shape, and often has a veil attached.

2-C42   MID 15TH CENTURY

An example of a shoe with pointed toe and small heel.

Early Renaissance

Renaissance, or the rebirth of the Classics, has its beginnings in Florence, Italy, in the 15th century. It is here that the wealthy patrons encouraged the arts and a humanistic approach to the Classics. Many of the wealthy patrons commissioned paintings and artwork to display their wealth and their adherence to the religious institution. In 1439, Gutenberg introduced the printing press and movable type printing, which was considered one of the most influential inventions of this period. Books were mass produced and literacy increased, especially for the middle class. The styles of Classical Greece and Rome were the catalyst for the design elements of the Early Renaissance.

Architecture / Furniture / Décor

Classical style and structure were revisited in Florence as architects searched for new direction. Because the Gothic style had not been fully accepted in Italy, the transition from that style to Classical was made much easier. Careful mathematical approaches to visual balance were incorporated into designs. The incorporation of the human factor rather than a heavenly goal appeared to be the main focus. Many classical elements such as coffered vaults, Corinthian columns and capitals, and the use of the dome, became regular features in architecture at this time. Furniture also began to adopt similar classical features from architecture. In addition, the development of a broader range of cabinet-type furniture from the traditional trunk were created to address a greater diversification of need from food storage, to clothing and plateware. Domestic structures began to incorporate fresco paintings as decoration on the interior walls.

Costume

Paintings become the most significant source of research for costumes worn by the wealthy and powerful. Portraits give us clear insight into the color and texture of the fabric, clothing, and accessory details, and the style of hair and makeup. Religious art was often reflective of the current style, even though they were depicting ancient times. The overall line of clothing reflected the natural draped silhouette of Classical Greece. Rich fabrics such as brocade, velvet, satin, and silk were used for the outer garments, while cotton and linen were used widely for the undergarments. The class system during this time was clearly defined, and sumptuary laws were passed to regulate the number of clothing articles a person could acquire based on their position in society.

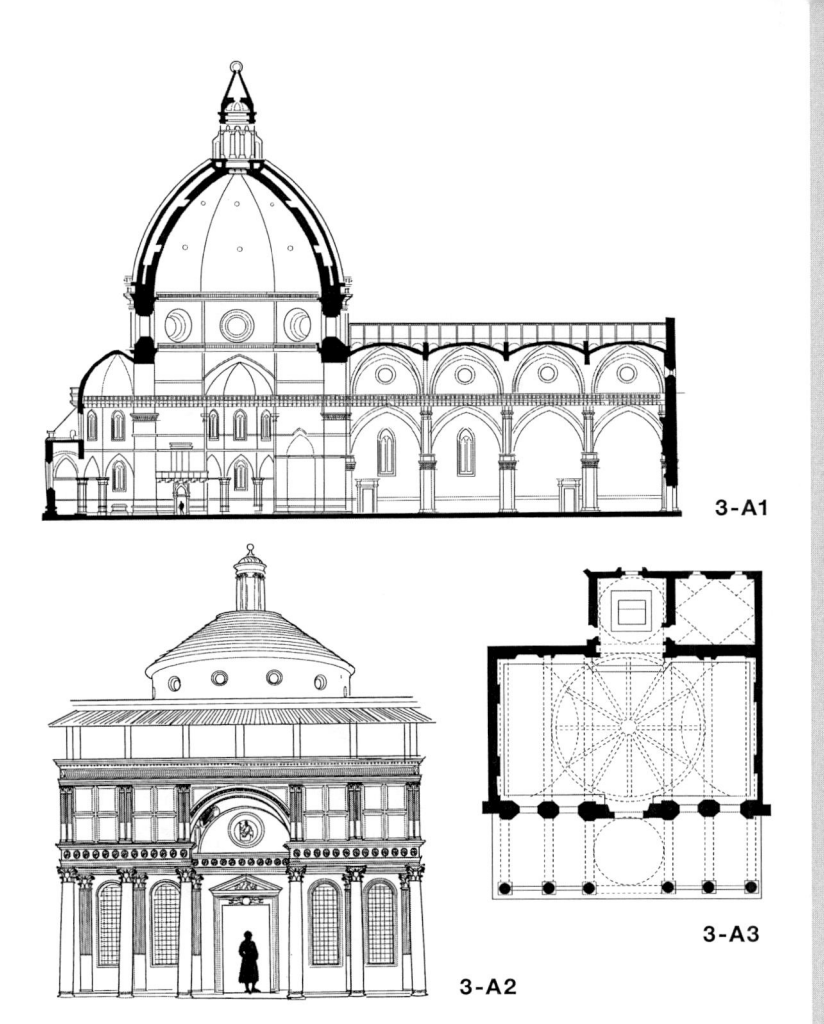

3-A1

3-A2

3-A3

3-A1 SECTION OF THE DOME OF SANTA MARIA DEL FIORE

The dome of Santa Maria del Fiore in Florence, Italy, was designed by Filippo Brunelleschi using elements of the Classical style. In addition, he designed the dome in two parts: an outer portion and an inner portion. This made the dome lighter and able to stand on the existing structure. 1436.

3-A2 PAZZI CHAPEL

The Pazzi Chapel located in Florence, Italy, was designed by Filippo Brunelleschi and contains many elements of classic Roman architecture. The building façade with its Corinthian columns is mathematically proportioned. 1443.

3-A3 PAZZI CHAPEL GROUND PLAN

As illustrated in the ground plan, the proportions of the interior and overhead dome have also been mathematically balanced.

3-A4

3-A4   BASILICA OF SANT'ANDREA MANTUA

Designed by Leon Battista Alberti, the Basilica located in Mantua, Lombardy (Italy) is patterned after a triumphal Roman arch. For this reason, the proportions on the façade, much like the Pazzi Chapel, are equally balanced using Classical elements. 1494.

3-A5   PALAZZO STROZZI

Built in Florence, Italy and designed by Benedetto da Maiano, the Palazzo Strozzi is made of rusticated stone with arched bifore windows. The ground floor has much smaller windows for security and visual purposes. 1489.

3-A6   PALAZZO STROZZI SECTION

As this section view of the Strozzi illustrates, the center of the structure has an atrium which is open to the sky. Balconies and rooms surround the atrium opening onto it. 1489.

3-A7   PALAZZO STROZZI GROUND PLAN

As illustrated here, the ground plan is based on an atrium design in which the center is open with multiple floors.

3-A8   COMPTON WYNYATES

Located in Warwickshire, England, Compton Wynyates is in the Tudor style. Originally a fortified structure with a moat and draw bridge, it was changed over time to be more of a manor house and less castle-like in its appearance. Elements of Tudor are the rambling nature of the structure, half-timbered gable ends to roofs, small leaded-glass windows, and different styles of chimneys. 1515.

3-A9   COMPTON WYNYATES GROUND PLAN

The rambling set of buildings and rooms around an open courtyard relate more to its history as a structure than to an intended appearance. Nonetheless, this approach was echoed by other manor houses of the period for the same historic reasons. Built around a courtyard from the beginning, rooms such as a great hall and gallery passages became elements of what would be referred to as the Tudor style.

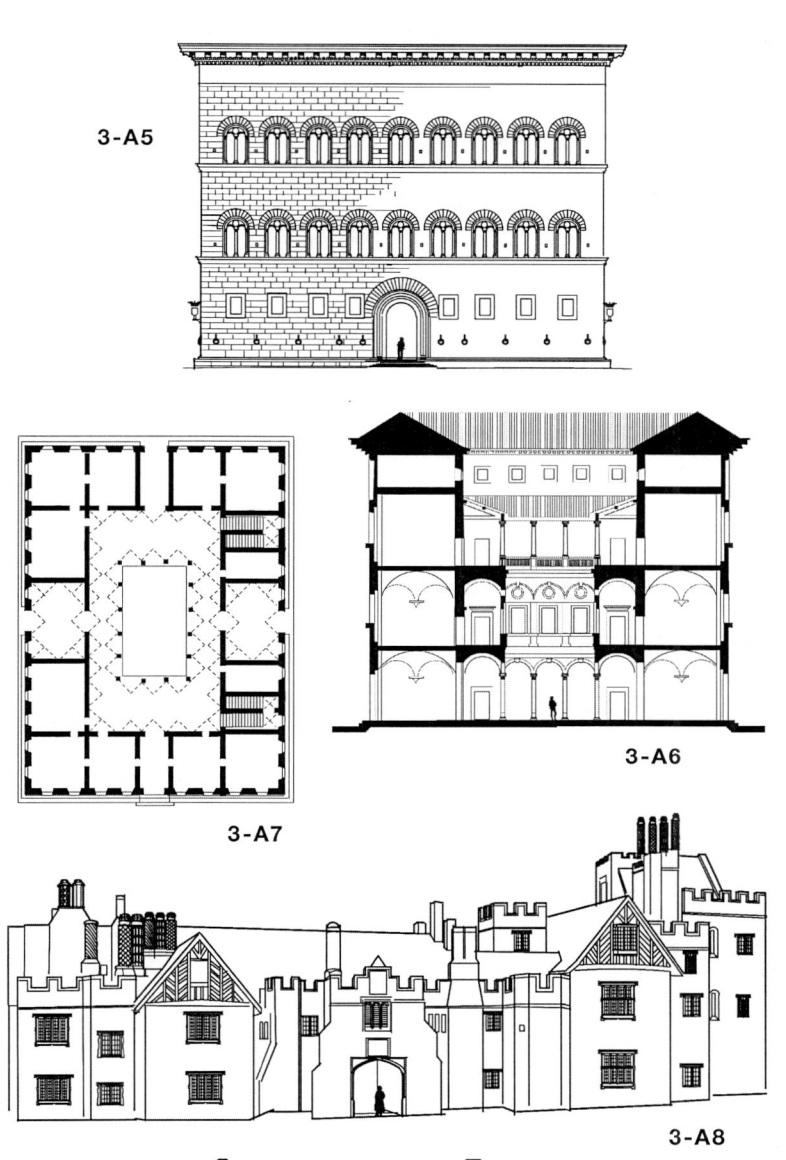

3-A5

3-A6

3-A7

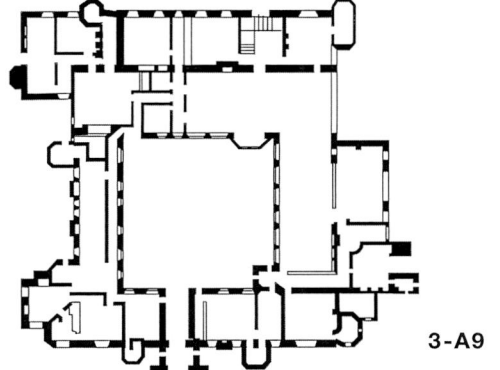

3-A8

3-A9

3-A10   HARDWICK HALL

This house was designed by Robert Smythson for Bess of Hardwick, in England. It is referred to as the "glass birdcage" because of the large windows. This was considered unusual to have such a large amount of wall space devoted to glass, which was very expensive. 1597.

3-A11   HARDWICK HALL GROUND PLAN

As illustrated in the Hardwick Hall ground plan, much of the outside walls are open to windows; chimneys were incorporated into the interior walls so that exterior wall space could be used for windows. The rooms are located around the Great Hall located in the center of the structure.

3-A10

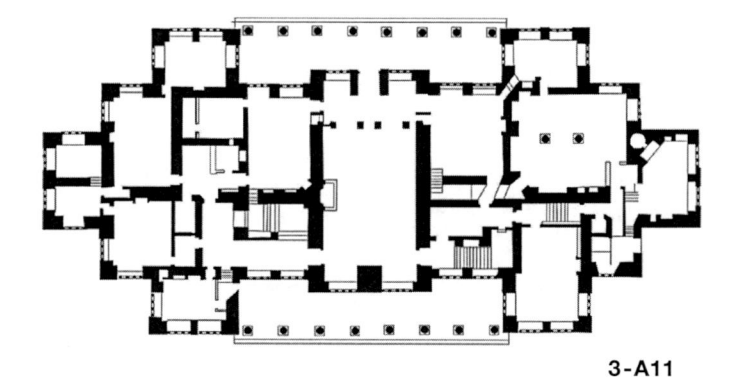

3-A11

3-A12 CHÂTEAU DE BLOIS

Château de Blois is located in the Loire Valley in France. Although the entire structure covers a time period from the 13th century to the 17th century, the section pictured here is from the time of Louis XII. Consisting of red brick and gray stone trim, the style has tall roofs and decorative wall dormers. 1515.

3-A13 CHÂTEAU DE BLOIS WINDOW DORMER DETAIL

The wall dormers of the Château de Blois are an extension of the wall area above the eave of the roof. These dormers can be heavily decorated with figures, faces, and tall extensions giving it a Gothic feel. Windows are generally stone mullions with leaded-glass inserts.

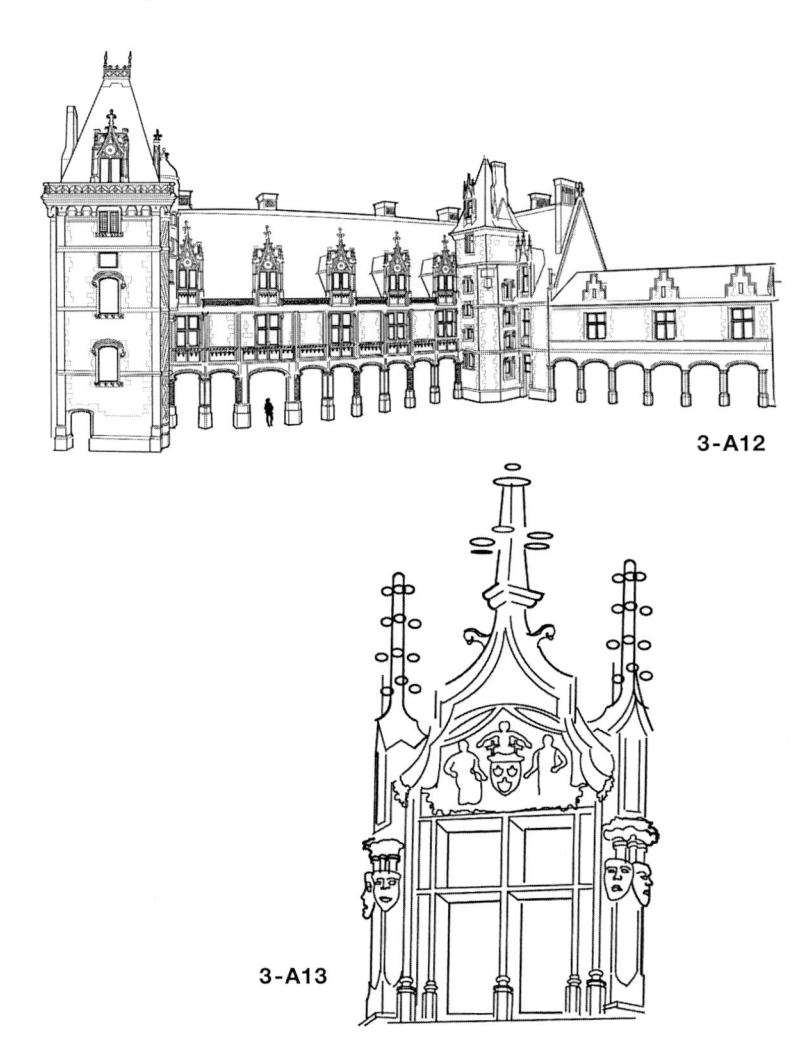

3-A12

3-A13

3-D1

3-D2

3-D1 NAVE OF BASILICA OF SANT'ANDREA, MANTUA
The nave of this basilica, designed by Leon Battista Alberti, has a coffered vault and side arches with classical pilasters. 1494.

3-D2 PAZZI CHAPEL
Filippo Brunelleschi designed this chapel using the square and circle. He incorporated classical elements and applied mathematics to determine scale and location. 1460.

3-F1

3-F2

3-F3

3-F5

3-F4

3-F1 CANOPY BED

This illustration of a canopy bed and side table was taken from a painting by Jan Van Eyck of the birth of John the Baptist. The bed is separate from the canopy and curtains. 1422.

3-F2 ITALIAN FOLDING CHAIR

Made from cypress wood. 15th century.

3-F3 SETTLE OR CHEST WITH BACK

This settle with arms has panels with linenfold relief and a seat that can be raised for storage. Late 15th century.

3-F4 SETTLE OR CHEST WITH MOVABLE BACK

This piece of furniture has arms, panels with linenfold relief, and a back that can be flipped to change direction. Late 15th century.

3-F5 SGABELLO CHAIR

Sometimes called the Strozzi, this chair is from Florence, Italy. The name refers to the fact that it is a three-legged stool with a crest of arms at the top of the back. 1491.

3-C1   C. 1450

State officials, lawyers, and older gentlemen wore the long gown, or surcote. The gown has tubular folds and wide sleeves. The tight-fitting sleeves of the doublet can be seen through the hanging sleeves of the gown. He is also wearing a coif under a chaperon which is a loose-fitted hat attached to a roundlet.

3-C2 & 3-C3   C. 1460

These two images illustrate the front and back view of a pleated surcote with sleeves that are fuller at the top and narrow at the wrist. The edge of the chemise is visible just below the sleeve edge. He is also wearing a flat brimmed hat, which was popular at that time.

3-C1

3-C4   C. 1495

The sleeveless outergarment with a V-shaped front and a pleated skirt is a jerkin. It is worn over a doublet with separate sleeves (upper and lower) that show off the chemise underneath. The drawers end above the knee and have points that connect these to the hose. The codpiece connects the separate legs of the drawers center front. The low-crowned hat and shoulder length hair were in fashion.

3-C5   C.1495

The doublet in this image is fitted to the torso with lacing up the front and detached sleeves allowing the chemise to be seen. He is wearing venetians, the earliest form of breeches, and the codpiece.

3-C6   C.1495

The doublet buttoned up the front with detached sleeves and was worn over the chemise. The hose is often fashioned of a left and right leg and as seen in this image connected together by points to the codpiece.

3-C7   C.1498

This is an example of a short gown, open in the front, with long tubular sleeves that is worn over a laced-up doublet, chemise, and hose. Shoes are broad-toed slippers without a heel.

3-C2

3-C3

3-C4

3-C5

3-C6

3-C7

3-C8

3-C9

3-C8   C.1485

Here is a closeup view of the doublet buttoned up the front with detached sleeves similar to 3-C6. He is also sporting the sugar loaf hat.

3-C9   C. 1498

In the latter part of the period, the doublet was often cut low to the waistline, with two-piece sleeves that opened at the elbow to allow the shirt to be seen. The low-neck shirt is evident in front and we can see the fullness from the shirred fabric attached to the yoke. A cord is used to attach the doublet front at the shoulders. The soft hat has a tassel on the end.

3-C10   C. 1520

This image provides a closeup view of the chemise that is being worn under the gown open in the front. The chemise is tightly gathered into a yoke and most likely made of linen.

3-C11   C. 1524

The gentleman is wearing an open gown over a doublet and chemise. The chemise is higher on the neck and a small ruffled collar appears. The sleeves get wider and fuller as we start the transition to the later Renaissance. Hairstyles later in the period are shorter for men.

3-C12   C.1527

This also provides an example of the chemise with a small standing collar. Over this is a full, pleated gown or surcote with wide sleeves. He is wearing a coif or fitted cap on his head. This hat is often worn under other hats. See 3-C16 and 3-C17.

3-C13   C. 1450

This is an example of a chaperon that has been wrapped around the head with a liripipe (a long tail of fabric) hanging in the back.

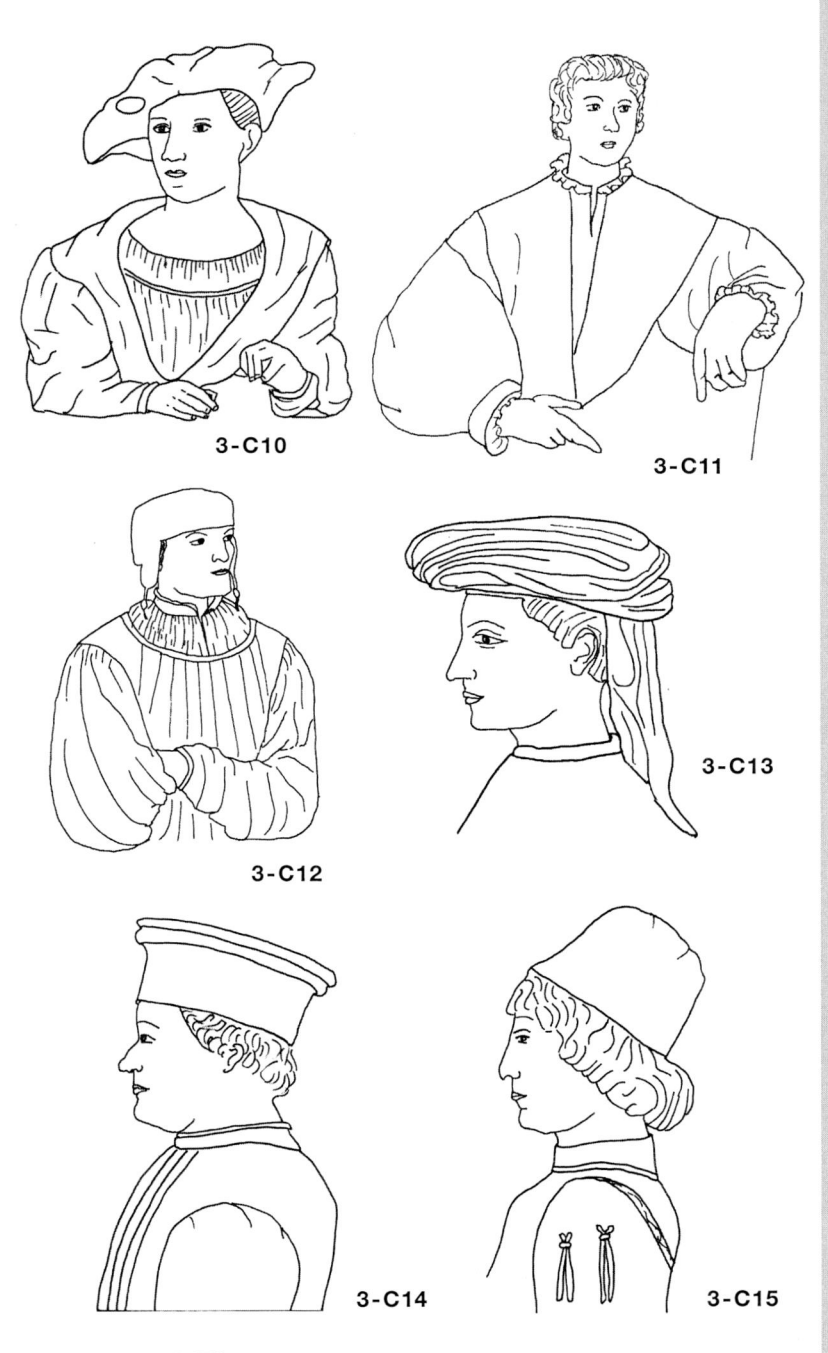

3-C10

3-C11

3-C12

3-C13

3-C14

3-C15

3-C14   C. 1470
The hat in this image is called a porkpie hat, a popular hat with Italian men during this time.

3-C15   C. 1470
The sugar loaf hat style, in the Gothic Period, continued to be worn during the early Renaissance.

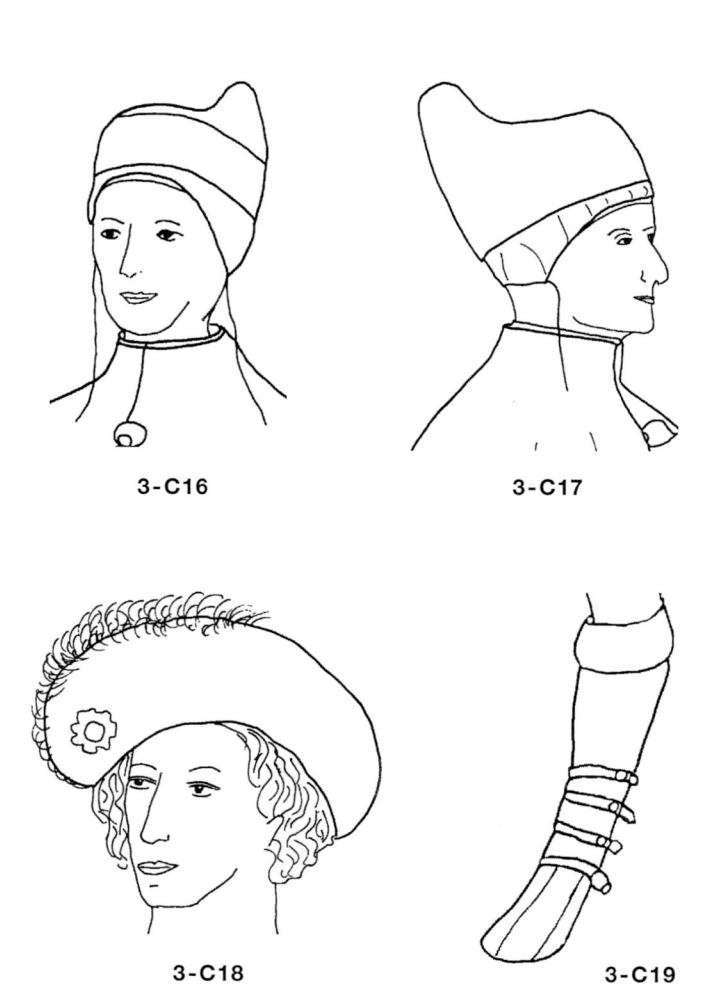

3-C16   **3-C17**

3-C18   **3-C19**

3-C16 & 3-C17   C. 1500

The Doge is both the religious leader and civic leader in Venice. These images show two views of the iconic hat, which is worn over the coif. The silhouette of this hat has similarities in shape to the pschent in Egypt. (See 1.C.7)

3-C18   C. 1510

This wide-brimmed hat with feathers continues to be a popular silhouette in the Late Renaissance period as well. They often applied jewelry such as brooches with stones on hats for decoration.

3-C19   C. 1500

The boot in this image is made of leather and typical of the style found in the Early Renaissance.

3-C20

3-C22

3-C21

3-C20 C.1495

The female silhouette reflects the soft, draped quality of the Greek silhouette in both dress and hair. The waist is worn high and under the bust with a wide belt, and the skirt is full and trains slightly in the back. The bodice is pleated in similar fashion to the male surcote, and the neckline is square.

3-C21 C.1495

The "V" or "U" shaped bodice on the gown, as in this drawing, often included a stomacher in the center or was worn to show the chemise or dress underneath. The detached sleeve, which is similar to the style of male doublets, allows more of the chemise to show.

3-C22 C.1498

The side view of this gown shows a drape, very similar to a Greek himation, over the high-waisted gown. The detached two-piece sleeves laced together, allowing the chemise to be pulled through and reflecting the curved draping of the Ionic chiton.

3-C23

3-C24

3-C25

3-C26

3-C23   C. 1450

This side closeup view of the bodice shows the pleating on the bodice similar to 3-C20. The sleeve of the gown is open in the middle from the shoulder to the wrist allowing the chemise sleeve to be prominent. The headpiece has two parts. There is a structured cap underneath, and a veil that is attached and draped in folds around the cap.

3-C24   C. 1470

The bodice in this image has a V-neckline with a center panel that is laced similar to the look of the laced doublets. It has tight-fitting detached sleeves. The hairstyle is pulled up on the side and curled.

3-C27

3-C28

3-C25   C. 1490

The bodice in this image has a square neckline with detached sleeves that have a fuller sleeve cap. The hair is pulled back with a jeweled hairband and tie. The hair could be in loose curls as in this image or worn in a braid encircled with ribbons.

3-C26   C. 1510

The back view of this gown shows a strip of fabric that is circling the garment. We have seen that strapping or girdling in the ancient Greek garments. Her hair is tied up with ribbons, and is similar to the style in 1-C45.

3-C27   C. 1520

As we move later in the period, the waistline is dropping closer to the natural waistline and is often worn with a decorative band around the waist. The sleeve design in this image, a wide upper sleeve that is gathered combined with a tighter lower sleeve, is very popular in the later Renaissance Period.

3-C28   C. 1530

The side view shows a bodice that appears to be high-waisted but much like the one above, there is a band around the waist making it more fitted at the waist unlike earlier in the period. The sleeves are two-piece and detached from the gown showing the chemise. The hat with feathers is similar to the male style seen in 3-C18.

3-C29   C. 1465

The hair and ornamentation were woven together to create hairstyles in this period. A circle of ribbons, feathers, and jewels are used to create the dramatic look. Pearls were commonly used in hair dressing.

3-C30   C. 1470

The henin, which made its debut during the Gothic period, continues to be worn in the Early Renaissance. In this image the henin has a velvet band that frames the face, in combination with a veil connected to a blunt tip. A black loop is seen on the center front forehead and believed to be either part of an undercap, or used for adjustment of the headpiece.

3-C31   C. 1490

This is another example of a henin, which is taller than the previous image with pointed tip. The veil in this image is attached to the base of the henin rather than the tip.

3-C32   C.1470

This style is referred to as a truncated henin because it is shorter than the typical henin and the top is wide and flat. There is also a veil, which is attached to the top and wrapped around the neck like a strap. During this time women would pluck their forehead to create a higher hairline. The signature black loop is evident in the center of her hairline.

3-C33   C.1490

The headpieces were often of several parts. There was likely a white coif underneath with the traditional black loop, and over this an outercap with a band of fabric to the shoulders that folded over to reveal the lining, which provided a contrasting color. The back piece of this headdress was a half-circle of fabric attached to the front band. The front band could be jeweled.

3-C34   C.1520

The headscarves, a carry-over from the Gothic period, are sometimes seen worn with a wimple or could be worn alone without the wimple as in this image.

3-C29

3-C30

3-C31

3-C32

3-C33

3-C34

Late Renaissance

The High, or Late Renaissance, begins in the 16th century, when the center of the Renaissance moves from Florence to Rome. It is also during this time period that other countries, such as England, Germany, France, and Spain begin to develop their own styles of the Renaissance. In addition to the interest in the arts and literacy, there were major changes in religious attitude. The Protestant Reformation divided Europe into two hostile religious camps, and these divisions fueled war between and within countries.

Architecture / Furniture / Décor

Although both Early and Late Renaissance styles incorporate Classical elements, the Late Renaissance in Italy creates a greater sophistication in the use of these elements. Much of this reflects a time period of greater stability and trade. Palaces of the wealthy become much larger and more grand in design. Interiors incorporate frescoes reflecting the accomplishments of the owner and imply direct connections to religious figures. In countries outside of Italy, classical elements are incorporated, but yet removed a bit from a direct connection with the original classical structures. This enables countries like France and England to include local elements and symbols with the Classical, to create their own version of Renaissance style.

Costume

The natural silhouette of the Early Renaissance transitions into a more structured and artificial silhouette, caused by wired understructures and padding. The early part of this century is often referred to as the Tudor Period, named after Henry VIII of England. It is distinguished by broad shoulders and a square shape, and has a strong German influence. Farthingales and corsets to control a woman's figure make their appearance. The second half of the century is often referred to as the Elizabethan period after Elizabeth I. Spain's influence is felt during the later years, as the silhouette becomes more vertical in line, and unnatural padding distorts the shape of the body. In addition to paintings, which continue to provide a wealth of information, actual garments survive from this time period and are a valuable research tool.

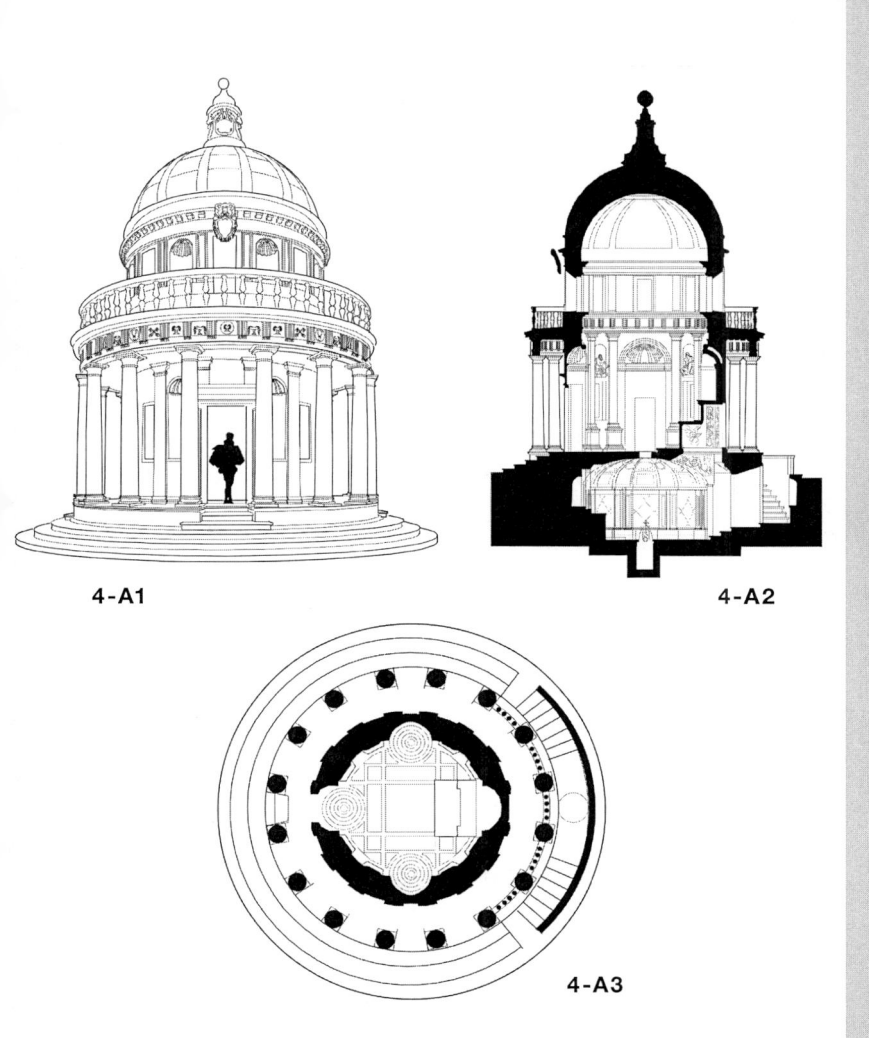

4-A1

4-A2

4-A3

4-A1   TEMPIETTO

The Tempietto, or small temple, was designed by Donato Bramante in Rome, influenced by the Temple of Vesta at Tivoli. 1502.

4-A2   TEMPIETTO SECTION VIEW

The elements that comprise the Late Renaissance style as represented in this structure are the circular ground plan, domed ceiling, and inclusion of classical elements such as Etruscan columns and trigliphs.

4-A3   TEMPIETTO GROUND PLAN

As illustrated in this ground plan, the Late Renaissance moves the plan layout from squares to circles, yet maintains a mathematical balance.

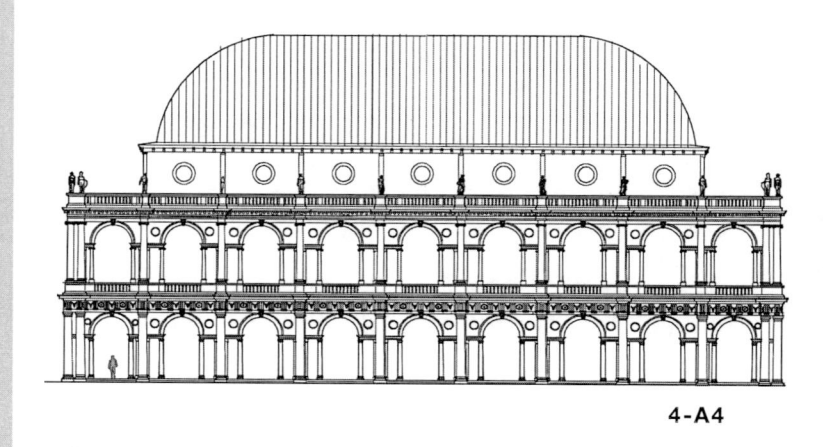

4-A4

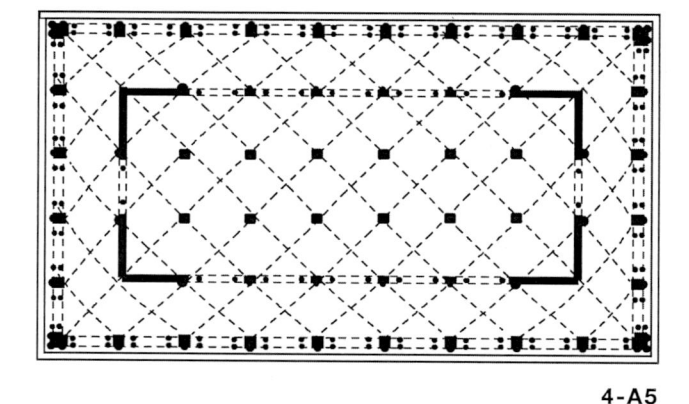

4-A5

4-A4 BASILICA PALLADIANA

This structure, designed by Andrea Palladio, is both a façade and supporting structure for the older building it surrounds. The classical elements are used to mask buttresses that help support the vaulted ceiling without looking like buttresses. 1549.

4-A5 BASILICA PALLADIANA GROUND PLAN

Located in Vicenza, Italy, the Loggia, designed by Andrea Palladio, surrounds the original structure. 1549.

4-A6 BASILICA OF ST. PETER

Located in Rome, the Basilica of St. Peter expands upon the principles of the dome, the coffered vault, and a balanced cross ground plan. Although during its long development stage many notable designers were involved, Michelangelo is credited with the most significant elements. Begun in 1502, it was not completed until 1626.

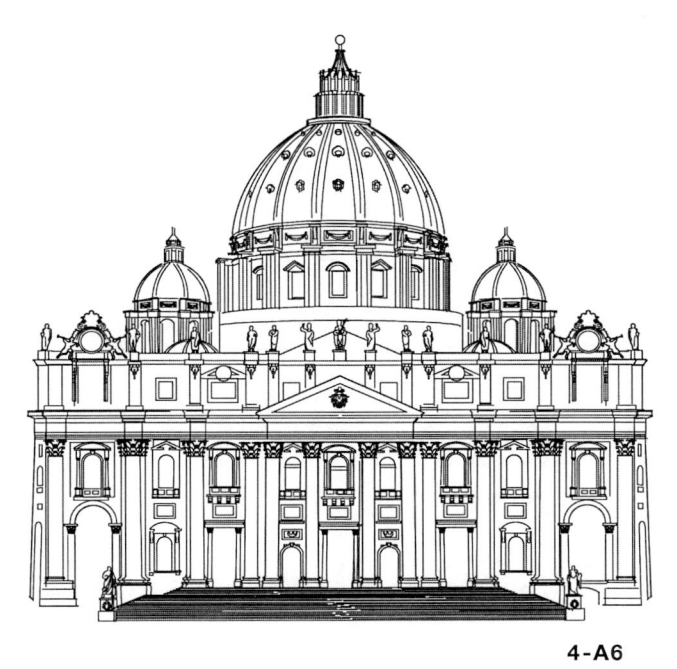

4-A6

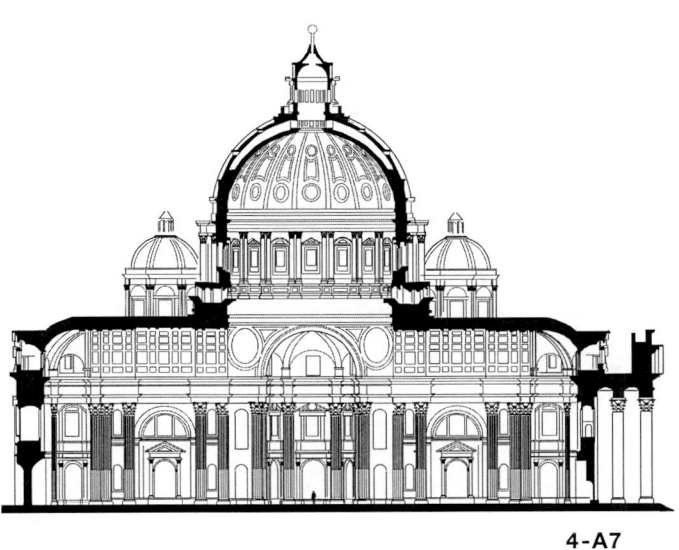

4-A7

4-A7   SECTION VIEW OF ST. PETER'S BASILICA

The section view of the Basilica is based on a Greek cross ground plan. The large dome rests on a drum of clerestory windows that is supported by four large piers. The use of dual columns in pairs is a recurring visual theme in Michelangelo's design.

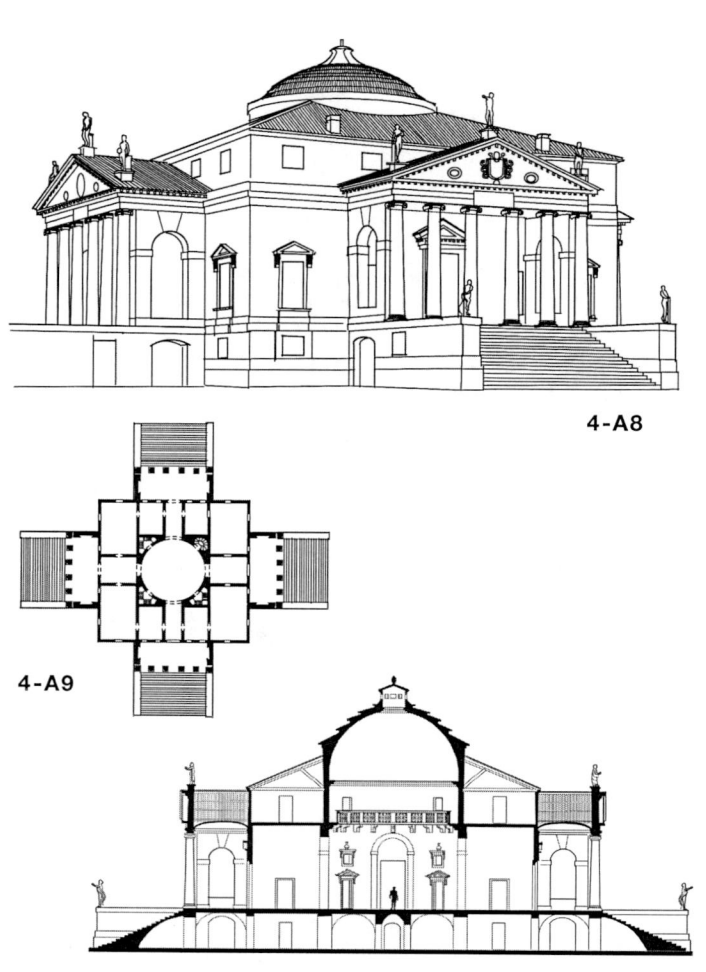

4-A8

4-A9

4-A10

4-A8   VILLA ROTONDA

Designed by Andrea Palladio, the Villa Rotonda has a ground plan
that is considered bisymmetrical, which means all four sides of the
exterior are the same, including steps and an Ionic pillared portico.
1566.

4-A9   VILLA ROTONDA GROUND PLAN

As pictured here, the layout of the structure is bisymmetrical. In
true Renaissance style, this ground plan is in perfect geometrical
balance.

4-A10   VILLA ROTONDA SECTION VIEW

As seen in this section view, the main rooms of the house are on
the first floor with the center area open up to the dome. Additional
bedrooms are on the second floor and servants' quarters and
kitchen are on the lowest floor.

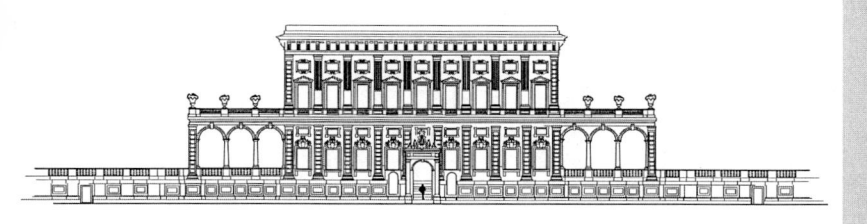

4-A11

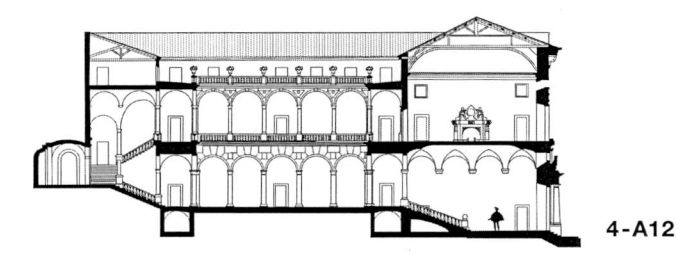

4-A12

4-A11   PALAZZO DORIA-TURSI

The Palazzo, located in Genoa, was designed by Giovanni and Domenico Ponzello in the mid 16th century. It contains many Classical elements such as fluted pilasters on the second floor and rusticated stone pilasters on the first floor, as well as pediments over the windows.

4-A12   SECTION VIEW OF THE PALAZZO DORIA-TURSI

This structure was constructed with the concept of visual avenues leading from the main entrance, ascending a grand staircase to the atrium, and then more elaborate stairs to the rest of the structure. It is surrounded by three gardens of which the back garden is raised to a higher level than the front of the structure.

4-A13

4-A13   FRANCIS I STAIRCASE

The staircase, located at the Château de Blois, is in the French Renaissance style. 1515.

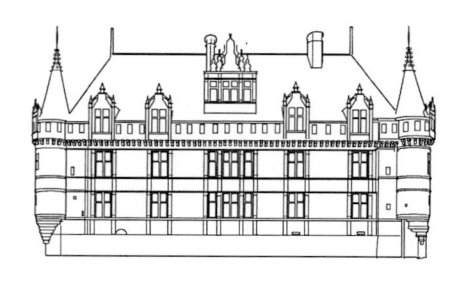

4-A14

4-A15

4-A16

4-A14   CHÂTEAU D'AZAY-LE-RIDEAU

This château is located on an island in the Indre River on the sight of a 13th century castle. This new structure, although built reflecting much of the new Italian Renaissance style, contains castle elements such as turrets, but also contains wall dormers of the French style. 1527.

4-A15   CHÂTEAU DE CHAMBORD

This chateau is in the Frances I style and is considered both Renaissance combined with Medieval styles. Designed as a castle with a moat and wall, its function is less defensive and more of a stylistic choice. It contains the tall roofs and wall dormers popular in French architecture of this time. 1547.

4-A16   BURGHLEY HOUSE

Burghley House is considered a vision of Renaissance proportion and a strong example of 16th century masonry. Located in England, the structure is built around a center courtyard and seen as an example of late Elizabethan style. 1587.

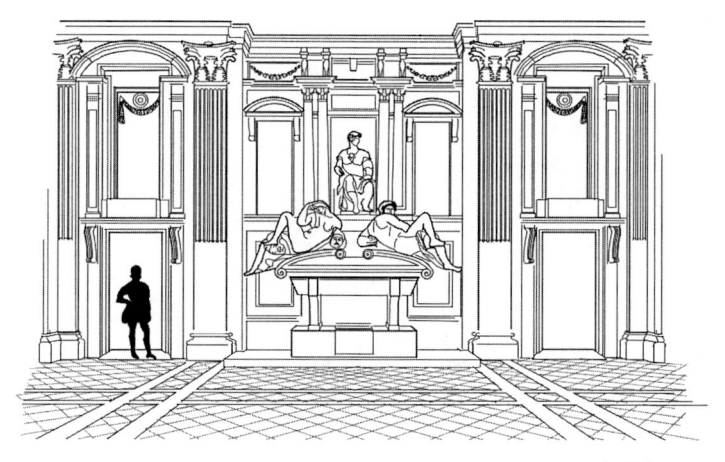

4-D1

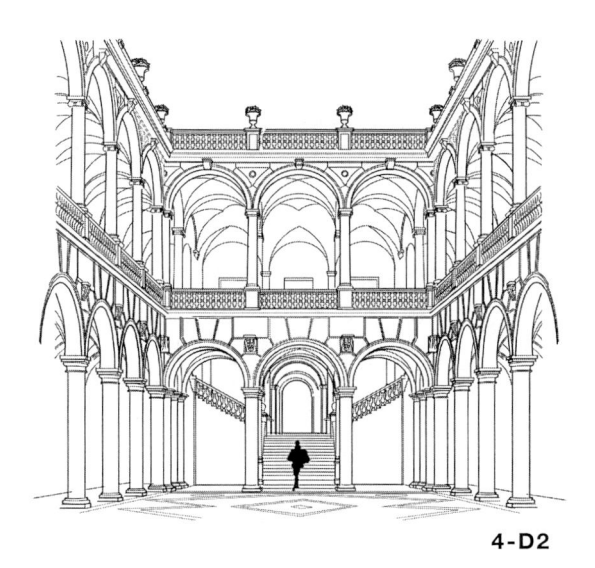

4-D2

4-D1 MEDICI CHAPEL

This chapel was created by Michelangelo and is located in San Lorenzo in Florence, Italy. Michelangelo only finished two of the tombs. They possess significant elements of his interior style: tabernacle windows, fluted dual pilasters, and figures carved in classical poses. 1533.

4-D2 ATRIUM OR CORTILE OF THE PALAZZO DORIA-TURSI

The view in the Palazzo Doria-Tursi is from the top step of the vestibule looking into the atrium, or cortile. Classical arches and columns are used with vaulted ceilings to give the space an open-air feel, in order to create vistas that draw the viewer into the space.

99

4-D3

4-D4

4-D5

4-D6

4-D3   CHÂTEAU DE FONTAINEBLEAU GALLERY OF FRANCES I
In this gallery, artists and sculptors from Italy were brought to
France to produce renovations in the new Renaissance style. A
dado located one-third of the way up the wall has wood paneling
with heraldic devices in low relief. Above this dado are paintings
illustrating the magnificence of Frances I framed by high-relief
sculpted figures. This hall is considered the first true introduction
of the new Renaissance style in France. 1539.

4-D4   DETAILS OF THE GALLERY OF FRANCES I
This gallery is considered part of the Mannerist style, which comes
from the Italian word "maniera," meaning style. It refers to the
transition between the idealized elements of the Renaissance and
the theatricality of the Baroque styles.

4-D5   DETAILS OF THE GALLERY OF FRANCES I CEILING
The design of this ceiling is comprised of small geometric beveled
panels between the ceiling beams. It is considered part of the
French Renaissance style.

4-D6   GRAND STAIRCASE AT KNOLE HOUSE
The grand staircase at Knole House in England is considered
a very good example of English Renaissance style, combining
elements of Italian Renaissance in three-dimensional work with
flat painted elements. As an example, the railing and spindles are
real on one side of the stairs, but are painted on the opposite side
on the flat wall to match the three-dimensional side. This style
also used geometric designs painted onto both flat and three-
dimensional structure. 1603.

101

4-D7

4-D8

4-D7   GREAT HALL OF HATFIELD HOUSE

This Great Hall is considered a transition from the Elizabethan to the Jacobean styles. The tapestry and wood screen along with the pronounced hearth are part of the Elizabethan style, and the wood-paneled walls and coffered ceiling are part of the Jacobean style.

4-D8   GREAT CHAMBER OF HARDWICK HALL

The Great Chamber of Hardwick Hall in England uses wall paintings and tapestries as the main wall covering. The frieze area of the wall is a forest scene with the court of Diana, incorporating scenes of country life and animals. 1597.

Sell your books at sellbackyourBook.com!

Go to sellbackyourBook.com and get an instant price quote. We even pay the shipping - see what your old books are worth today!

00067640847

0006764 **0847** C-3 3

4-F2

4-F1

4-F3

4-F1   CAQUETOIRE CHAIR

This is a conversational chair designed to accommodate women's wide skirts. For this reason, the front of the chair is much wider than the back. The backs are usually taller with panels and possibly medallions. 16th century.

4-F2   COURT CUPBOARD

This English cupboard, popular throughout the 16th century, was used as a buffet or to display plateware. The supports are typically English and are referred to as a "cup and cover" with a scroll connecting it to the table-type top.

4-F3   FRENCH ARMOIRE

The French armoire consisted of an upper piece that had two doors and drawers and a lower piece, also with two drawers and doors. Decorations consisted of Romantic and heroic scenes along with terminus and architectural elements. Mid 16th century.

4-F4

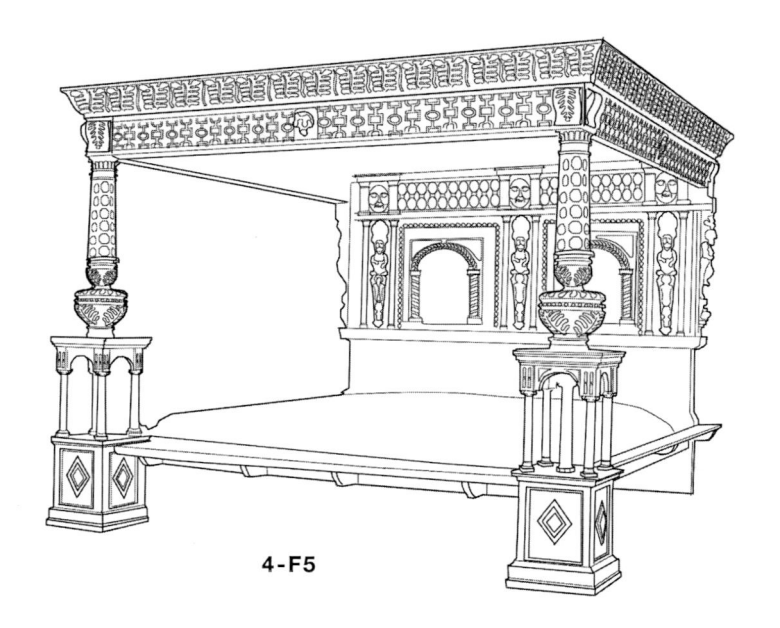

4-F5

4-F4   FRENCH SAMBIN TABLE

This table has been created by one of the schools of design in France. It is richly carved, with motifs of chimeras, caryatides, colonnades, and arcades.

4-F5   GREAT BED OF WARE

Originally located in the White Hare Inn in Hertfordshire, it consists of a cup and cover supporting the canopy and terminus on the headboard with architectural elements. Dates from 1590.

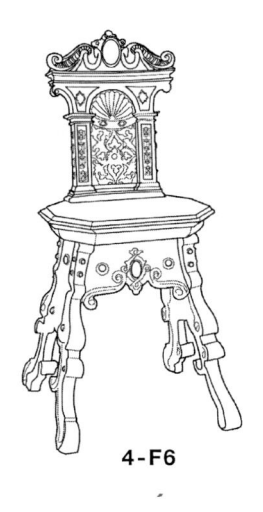

4-F6

4-F7

4-F8

4-F6   BACK OR SLAB STOOL

The back or slab stool was carved by Giovanni Maria Nosseni.
The basic slabs that make up the chair are heavily carved with
architectural elements. 1580.

4-F7   THE SGABELLI CHAIR

This chair, which is similar to the slab chair, has the carved
supports on the front and back of the chair. Latter half of the
16th century.

4-F8   ITALIAN CHEST OR CASSONE

This Italian Renaissance chest is carved from walnut, with
terminus figures on the corners and lions' paws for feet. Mythical
figures are carved in low relief. 16th century.

4-C1

4-C2

4-C3

4-C1 C. 1530

The male silhouette shifts from vertical and slim to a horizontal broad silhouette as we move into the Tudor Period. The outerwear in this image is a short gown, with a wide fur collar and short puffed sleeves. The doublet has a short skirt and slashed sleeves. The hose could be in two pieces and referred to as the upper stocks and lower stocks. The upper stocks were often slashed as well as the sleeves. The hat is also broad and low, often ornamented with an ostrich feather.

4-C2 C. 1530

This image provides a closeup view of the slashing used on both the doublet front and sleeves. The collar is moving from the low open collar, which revealed more of the shirt underneath to a standing collar.

4-C3 C. 1535

The jerkin follows the shape of the doublet, and is more of a jacket, which can be sleeveless or with sleeves. In this image the jerkin has wings (short cap sleeves), which allow the doublet sleeves to show underneath. The hairstyles of men in this century become shorter and beards are common. The hat has a small brim with a feather.

4-C4

4-C5

4-C4   C. 1533

Gowns could be either the fashionable short gowns (see 4-C1) or long gowns, which were worn by lawyers, religious leaders, and professional men. The four-cornered brimless hat, which we see here, is the prototype of modern academic headwear.

4-C5   C. 1540

Religious attire consists of the long gown and wide sleeves (chasuable) over an undertunic/gown with narrow sleeves. A close-fitting cap is worn on the head.

4-C6

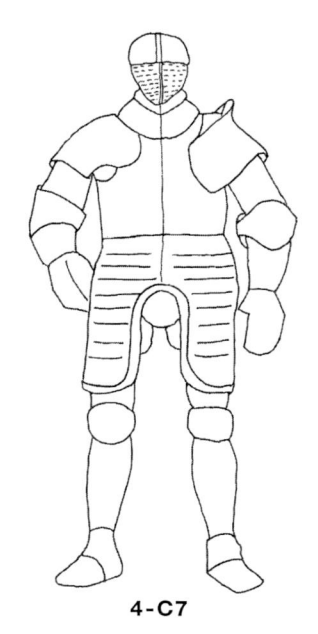

4-C7

4-C6   C. 1536

The style of Henry VIII favored an extreme boxy silhouette. In this iconic image, he is wearing a slashed doublet, the U-shaped jerkin with a pleated skirt that hangs to above the knee, and a short gown with wide fur collar. The neckline of the doublet is wide and reveals the chemise. He is wearing garters below the knee, holding up the lower stocks. His shoes echo the broad silhouette and are slashed. The hat is wide and low with feathers on the edge of the brim.

4-C8

4-C7   C. 1540

The armor in this image was also worn by Henry VIII, which gives us some idea of his actual size and shape. In contrast to the 4-C5, it is slim and tall. The codpiece is included in the design of armor.

4-C8   C. 1550

This image illustrates dress armor worn over upper stocks with broad-toed shoes. The armor has a similar silhouette to the doublet shape and follows fashion with the inclusion of the codpiece.

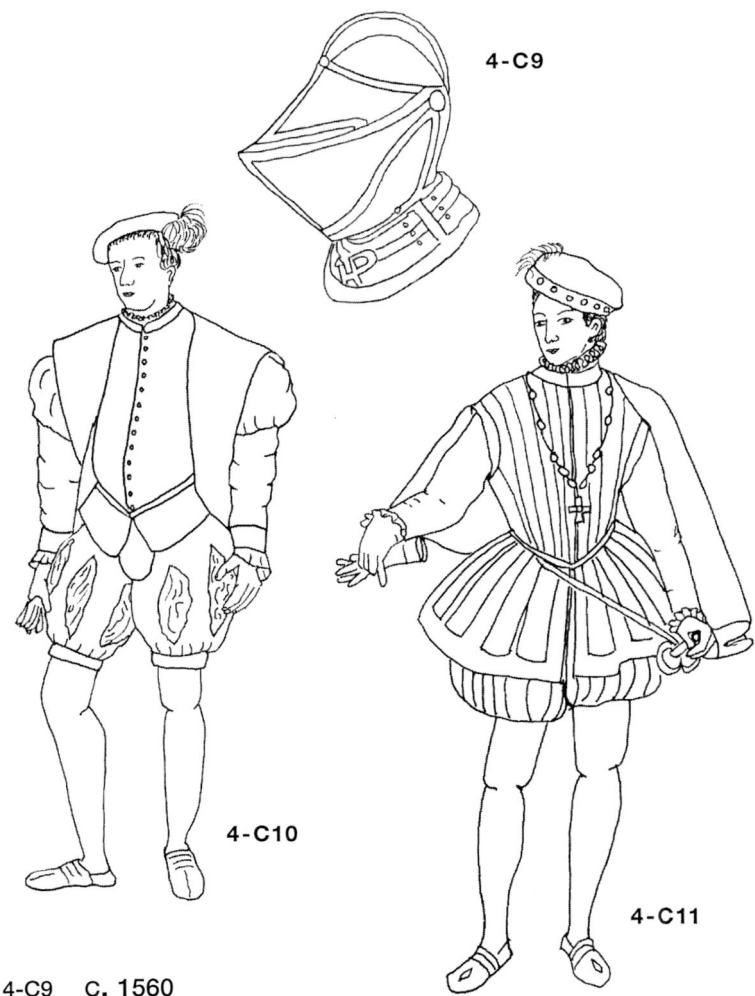

4-C9

4-C10

4-C11

4-C9   C. 1560

An example of a helmet style.

4-C10   C. 1548

The peascod belly doublet in this image is padded in the stomach area using bombast. This fashion continues through the end of the century. The upper stocks have panes of contrasting fabric that are sewn into the slashes. The lower stocks are fitted and attached to the upper stocks. The codpiece on the upper stocks is mostly a fashion statement and it becomes more padded during the latter half of the century.

4-C11   C. 1566

The jerkin or jacket is fitted to the doublet shape and is sleeveless with wings, allowing the doublet sleeves to show. The upper stocks are getting fuller and padded, and are referred to as melon or pumpkin hose. The short cape replaces the short gown as outerwear.

4-C12

4-C13

4-C14

4-C12   C. 1570

Pumpkin breeches are at their widest in the latter part of the
century. They often required padding to maintain their shape. The
doublet in this image shows a series of small slashes throughout.
The standing collar has a small ruffled edge.

4-C13   C. 1588

In the latter part of the century the upper stocks or breeches
become very short. They are combined with tight-fitting breeches
known as canions that are worn underneath. The hose or lower
stocks are fitted and often made of silk. This youth is sporting the
peacod belly doublet and a wired large ruff along with a cape.

4-C15

4-C16

4-C17

4-C18

4-C14   C. 1600

At the end of the century the breeches are full but less padded. They are combined with canions that tie at the knee using garters. The jerkin has wings at the shoulders and a short peplum. This is worn over the doublet and a small ruff finishes the neck. The hat is taller and sports a larger brim.

4-C15   C. 1570S

This gentleman sports a small ruff that sits above the standing collar of the jerkin. Late century, the hats are taller but still include a feather as ornamentation.

4-C16   C. 1587

This is an example of a wider ruff that sits on the shoulder.

4-C17   C. 1530S

This stub-toed shoe is an example of the style earlier in the century, more specifically in the Tudor period.

4-C18   C. 1560S

Later in the time period the shoes have rounded toes. Some of them had straps going across to secure them to the feet.

4-C20

4-C21

4-C19

4-C19　C. 1553

The Tudor style for women includes a cone-shaped silhouette that is supported by a Spanish farthingale (a hooped underskirt that was bell shaped). The neckline is square, similar to the male style of the same time. The undergown (referred to as a petticoat) has full sleeves, gathered in at the wrist with slashes that allow the chemise to show. The overgown has wide sleeves trimmed in fur. The pomander, a filigree ball with fragrances, hangs from the jeweled girdle.

4-C20　C. 1536

The woman in this image is wearing a gabled headdress with a hood that holds the hair. The neckline is square and embellished with jewels and precious stones. The sleeves, which are now sewn into the gown, consist of the wide three-quarter sleeves of the gown, and split sleeves of the petticoat which are tied to allow the tufts of the chemise to show through.

4-C21　C. 1546

The sleeves on the undergown in this image are made up of panes of fabric tied together to allow the chemise to show through. The overgown has hanging sleeves. She is wearing a French cap, which was a crescent-shaped headpiece trimmed in pearls. It was held onto the head using a strap.

4-C22

4-C23

4-C24

4-C22   C. 1540S

The bodice in this gown is a departure from the square neckline, and has a large open standing collar that exposes the lining. A small pearl necklace is worn on the open neckline while a larger pendant hangs from the center of the collar. The ruffle of the chemise, which could be embroidered in blackwork, is seen at the wrist. The leg of mutton sleeves seen in this image will gain popularity during the century. She is wearing a French hood headpiece with a short panel at the back with a circle of pearls at the back.

4-C23   C. 1550

The square neckline has a sheer embroidered partlet that is gathered into the neck, which creates a small ruffle at the neckline and is the forerunner of the ruff that we see later in the century. It was in fashion to drape pearls on the bodice. The bodice was kept smooth by use of a vasquine, heavily boned understructure, which is a forerunner of the corset. The sleeves on petticoat feature short multiple puff sleeves worn underneath the slashed sleeve on the gown.

4-C24   C. 1530

This image is a closeup view of the simpler gabled headdress without the hood. The headpiece was structured and framed the face, and was a popular style in the Tudor period.

113

4-C26

4-C25

4-C25   C. 1555

As we move into the mid-century, the silhouette becomes more vertical. The gown has the square neckline, the bodice dips to a point below the waist, and the sleeves become more tapered. Short puffs at the shoulder are combined with a more fitted lower sleeve. The skirt on the gown maintains the bell-shaped silhouette from before but has more fullness.

4-C26   C. 1563

The skirts become wider as we move through the century. The neckline is slightly curved and she is wearing a sheer partlet on the upper bodice. The sleeves have quite a few slashes in which the chemise has been pulled through to create small puffs. Around her waist is a jeweled girdle with perhaps a reliquary at the base.

4-C27   C. 1569

This image is based on a portrait of Queen Elizabeth I. Over the gown, she wears a robe with a train. The crown and orb are symbols of the monarch.

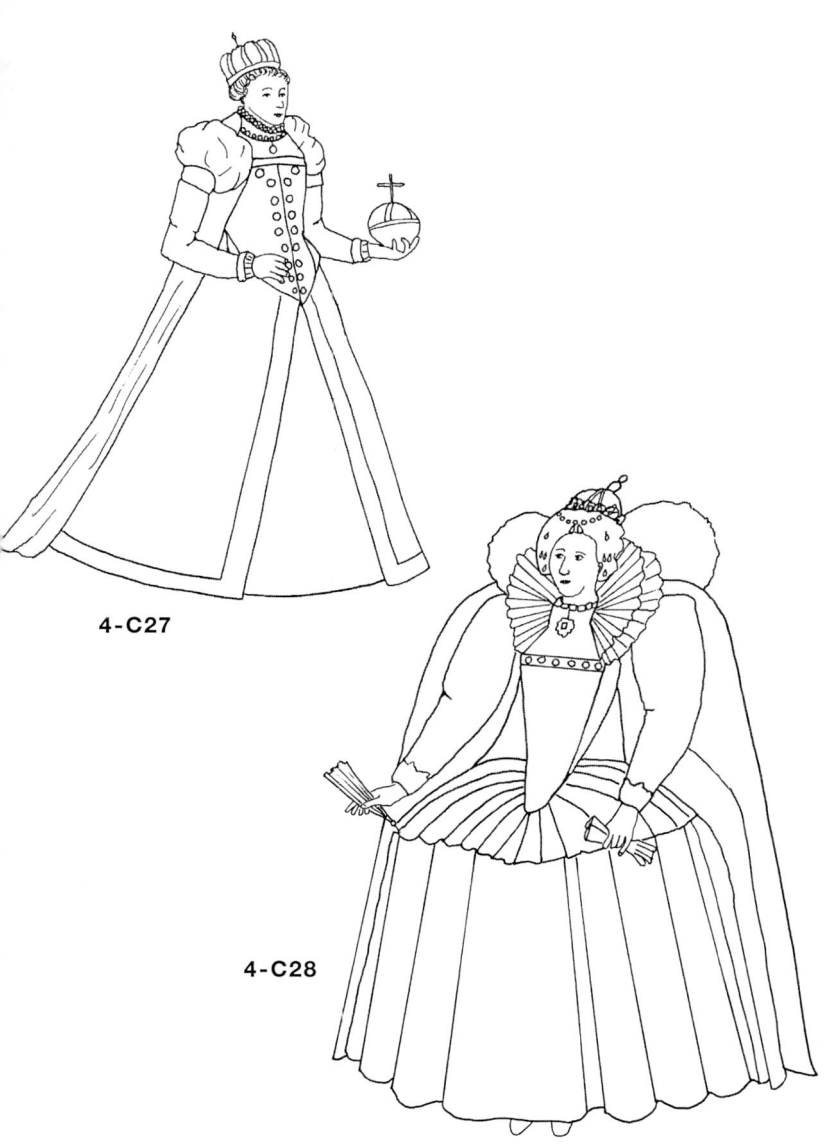

4-C27

4-C28

4-C28   C. 1592

The famous image of the coronation of Queen Elizabeth I
illustrates the silhouette created by the understructure known
as the French or cartwheel farthingale. This was a drum-shaped
wired or caned underskirt that supported the gown. The
stomacher dipped below the waist and was supported by
corsets made of iron. The leg-of-mutton sleeves are very wide
at the shoulder and become narrow at the wrist. She is wearing
a French inspired open high-standing ruff, which is supported
by an underpropper. The back of the costume is framed by a
whisk (high circular sheer panels, edged in lace) that creates a
background for her crown and hair, adorned with pearls.

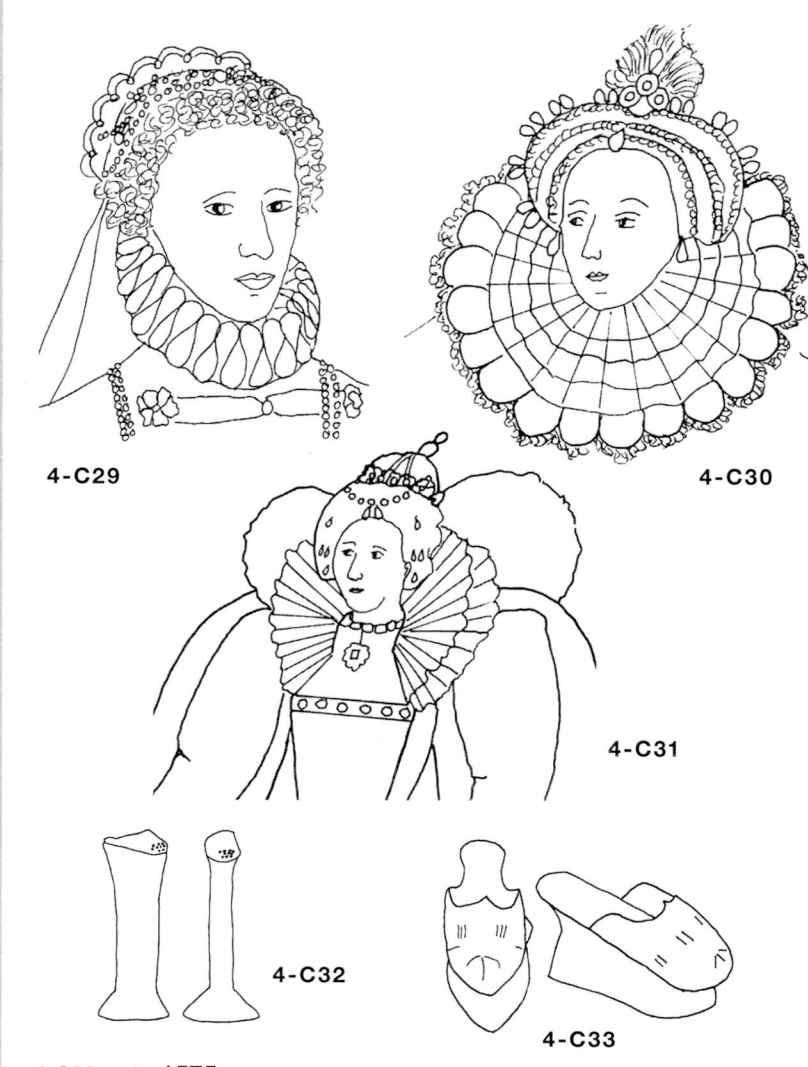

4-C29

4-C30

4-C31

4-C32

4-C33

4-C29   C. 1575

Women as well as men wore ruffs on the neck, which were pleated linen collars attached to a band. They varied in size and shape. Starch was used to give the folds crispness.

4-C30   C. 1588

This woman is wearing a wide ruff edged in lace. The width of the ruff requires wired support by the underpropper.

4-C31   C. 1592

This is a closeup view of the open high-standing ruff and whisk. (See 4-C28) The depth of the ruffs could be between 6"–8".

4-C32 & 4-C33   C. 16TH CENTURY

These are two versions of chopines, a high-heeled shoe worn by women in the Late Renaissance. Traditionally they were between 6"–15" but could be higher.

17th Century

The 17th century, also known as the Baroque Period, is marked by two significant influences: the Catholic Church's attempt to win back those lost to the Reformation by a grand building plan, and the rise of royal patronage through rulers, such as Louis XIV of France, who impacted all aspects of the Arts. The Court of Versailles, created by Louis XIV, became the center of upper class activity, and established a grandeur that inspired other European monarchs.

Architecture / Furniture / Décor

Louis XIV was a significant supporter of the arts. Palaces, like that of Versailles, were envied and replicated across Europe. At Versailles, academies such as Gobelins were created for the training, and creation, of everything from architecture to tapestries, painting and sculpture. These academies attracted some of the best artists in Europe and enabled France to be the center of the arts in the 17th century. For the first time, all aspects of architecture, furniture, gardens and décor were coordinated, and visually revolved around an overarching theme. The use of marquetry and the inlay of exotic materials were accelerated to a high art form.

Costume

The Late Renaissance fashion extends into the early part of this century for England, France, and Germany. Spain holds onto the stiff, distorted Late Renaissance silhouette until later in the century. The Cavalier Period of fashion, in the first half of the century, brings back a high waistline inspired by the Greek silhouette, combined with a fanciful look enhanced by the use of lace, bows and feathers. This contrasts with the sober and simplistic garments of the Puritans, whose religious beliefs restrict the use of such adornments. In the second half of the century, there is a return to the natural waistline, but we continue to see the use of bows and lace on garments for both men and women. Men started to wear long curly wigs, and doublets are replaced by waistcoats and coats. Women begin to wear multiple petticoats to support the width of the skirt, and we see a forerunner to the bustle silhouette, which dominates the late Victorian period.

5-A1

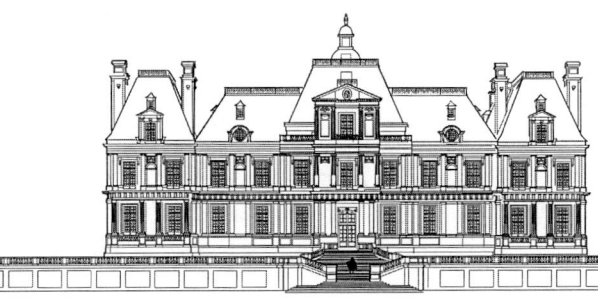

5-A2

5-A1   SAN CARLO ALLE QUATTRO FONTANE

The Church of San Carlo alle Quattro Fontane in Rome was designed by Francesco Borromini in the Baroque style. This style took the elements of the late Renaissance and created a greater three-dimensional dynamic. This can be seen in the convex/concave surface of the front of the church. 1646.

5-A2   CHÂTEAU DE MAISONS-LAFFITTE

The Château de Maisons near Paris, designed by François Mansart, uses classical elements such as pilasters and columns with Corinthian capitals to create a symmetrically balanced ground plan. A series of stairs and an avenue of gardens that one would pass through before entering was intended to give a feeling of grandeur. The roof, which is a style significant to Mansart, was created by removing the very top of the steep roof and capping it off with a decorative railing.1642.

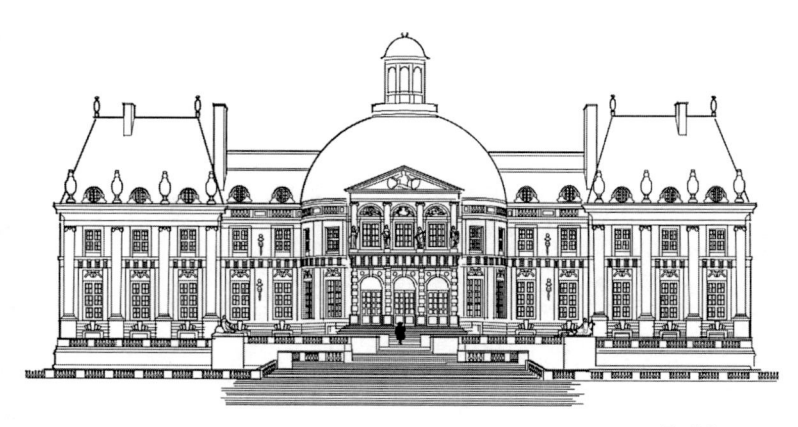

5-A3

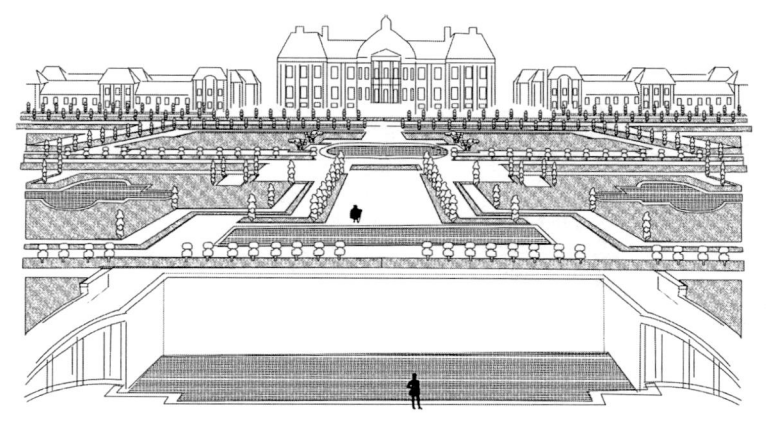

5-A4

5-A3 CHÂTEAU DE VAUX-LE-VICOMTE

Château de Vaux-le-Vicomte in Seine-et-Marne, France was designed by Louis Le Vau, with Charles Le Brun designing the interiors. The building is symmetrical, much like Château de Maisons, with an elliptical saloon. 1661.

5-A4 CHATEAU DE VAUX-LE-VICOMTE GARDENS

Designed by André Le Nôtre, the Château de Vaux-le-Vicomte gardens are symmetrical along a central axis. Le Nôtre also employed a subtle forced perspective.

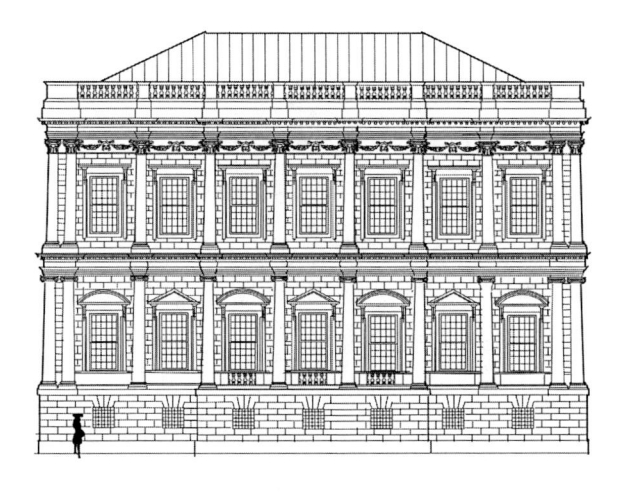

5-A5

5-A6

5-A5 BANQUETING HOUSE, WHITEHALL

The Banqueting House in London, designed by Inigo Jones in the Classical style, incorporates many Italian Renaissance elements such as classical columns in the Ionic style on the first floor and Corinthian style on the second. He also visually terminates the structure with a classical railing at the top. 1697.

5-A6 ST. PAUL'S CATHEDRAL

St. Paul's Cathedral in London was designed by Sir Christopher Wren in the Italian Late Renaissance style incorporating the use of double columns, double pilasters, tabernacle windows, and the drum and dome similar to St. Peter's Basilica in Rome. 1708.

5-D1

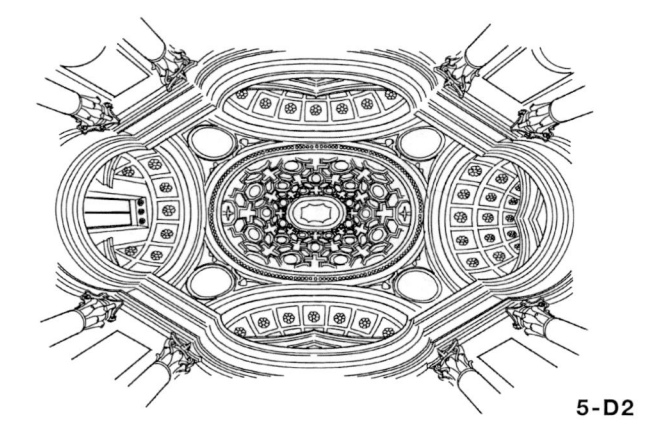

5-D2

5-D1 SANT'ANDREA AL QUIRINALE

The main altar of the Sant'Andrea al Quirinale details the Martyrdom of Saint Andrew. Designed by Guillaume Courtois, it is located in Rome. 1668.

5-D2 SAN CARLO ALLE QUATTRO FONTANE

The interior dome of San Carlo, located in Rome and designed by Francesco Borromini, is in the Baroque style. The view of this illustration is from the center looking up toward the oval-coffered dome. Below are the pendentives and the side-coffered arches, and below that is the main cornice that creates the opening in which all of this is seen, supported by Corinthian columns. 1646.

5-D3

5-D4

5-D5

5-D3   HALL OF MIRRORS AT VERSAILLES
The Hall of Mirrors is one of the grand passageways between apartments at Versailles in France. Designed by Charles Le Brun, it has arched windows along one wall and arched replicas of the windows on the other wall. The arched replicas have mirrors rather than glass. 1684.

5-D4   CANDELABRA DETAILS FROM THE HALL OF MIRRORS
The gilded candelabras from the Hall of Mirrors are carved and gilded with beveled crystal pieces and candles at the top. Many of the pieces were created to replace the solid silver originals.

5-D5   CHANDELIER DETAILS FROM THE HALL OF MIRRORS
Although not pictured in the illustration above, many crystal chandeliers are suspended from the ceiling. When lit, they not only illuminated the space, but the crystal pieces enable light to dance around the room, reflected by the many mirrors.

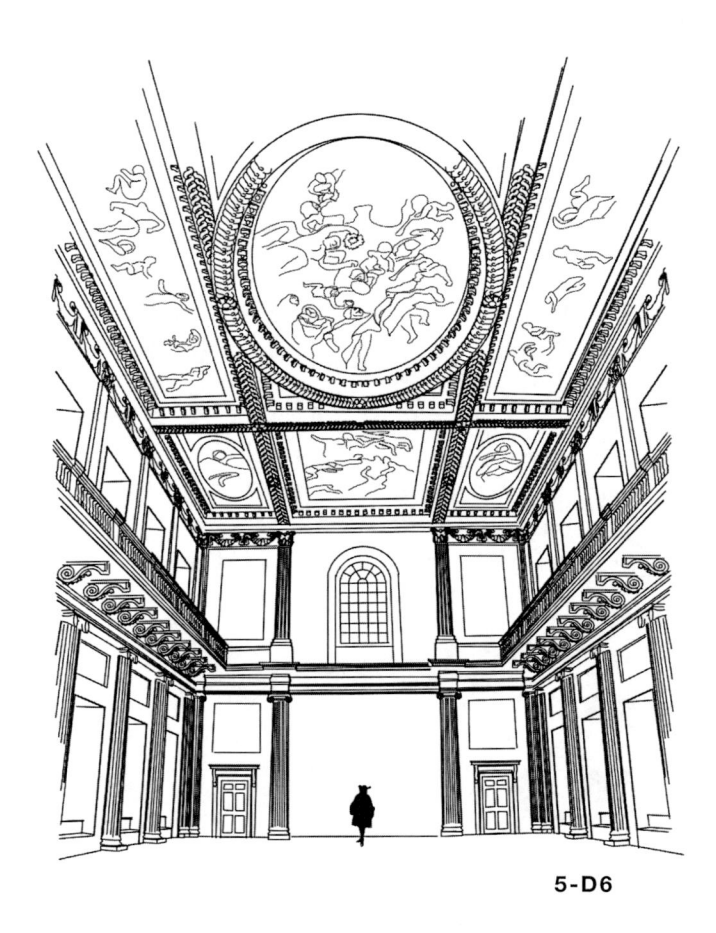

5-D6

5-D6 BANQUETING HOUSE

The Banqueting House is part of Whitehall, the royal palace designed by Inigo Jones, with Classical elements such as Ionic columns and capitals on the first level and Corinthian columns and pilasters on the second level. The ceiling has three paintings by Peter Paul Rubens in gilded frames. The general color scheme is white and gold. 1622.

5-F1

5-F2

5-F3

5-F4

5-F1   FARTHINGALE CHAIR
The Farthingale chair was designed to accommodate the farthingale skirt of the time. Considered Jacobean in style because of the tapestry and twist turn of the legs. Early 17th century.

5-F2   LOUIS XIII ARM CHAIR
The armchair is in the Louis XIII style with low back, legs and arms with beading spindles, and tapestry on the covering. Early 17th century.

5-F3   ENGLISH TABLE
This English table is in the Jacobean style with marquetry or inlay work, as well as the corkscrew-turned legs that were considered part of the style. Early 17th century.

5-F4   CAROLEAN DAYBED
This daybed is in the Charles I style with a carved wood frame and caning on the back and bed. The stretcher bars are heavily carved. Mid to Late 17th century.

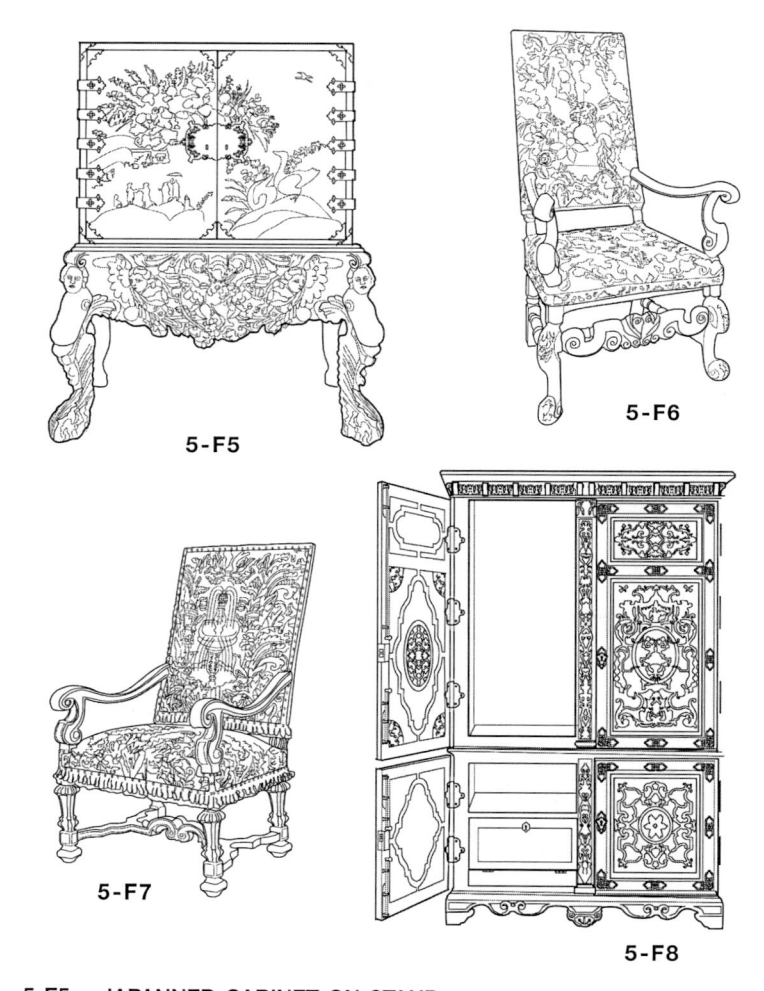

5-F5

5-F6

5-F7

5-F8

5-F5   JAPANNED CABINET ON STAND

This cabinet has a black lacquer finish with a painted scene and brass fittings. This was referred to as Japanning. The stand would be heavily carved and many times covered in silver leaf in a Baroque style. 1688.

5-F6   LOUIS XIV ARMCHAIR

This armchair is in the Louis XIV style, with a tall straight back, reverse or double scroll front legs, C-shaped arm supports and curved arm rests. Late 17th century.

5-F7   LOUIS XIV ARMCHAIR

This armchair is in the Louis XIV style with reverse scroll arm supports and straight square legs. 17th century.

5-F8   LOUIS XIV CUPBOARD

The cupboard is in the Louis XIV Baroque style, with brass mounts, ebony veneer, and marquetry. It is considered the work of André-Charles Boulle. 1700.

5-F9

5-F10

5-F12   5-F11

5-F9   LOUIS XIV WRITING DESK
This writing desk is in the Louis XIV style, with marquetry of brass, ebony, ivory, mother-of-pearl, copper, and pewter. Late 17th century.

5-F10   ENGLISH SECRETARY
The secretary is English in the William and Mary style, with a drop-down front, cabinet above, and Spanish feet below. Late 17th century.

5-F11   ENGLISH ARMCHAIR
This armchair with the tall back is considered in the William and Mary style, with its turned legs with Spanish feet. Scroll sides are English. Late 17th century.

5-F12   THE BRIGHTON BED
This English bed has red brocade curtains and a cover of silk. The oak frame has ostrich feathers on the canopy. 1670–1690.

5-C2

5-C1

5-C3

5-C1   C. EARLY 17TH CENTURY

In the early part of the century the style for men was similar to the late 16th century. The doublet and jerkin combination along with the ruff were worn. The pumpkin hose lost its padding and went to the knees. These breeches were sometimes referred to as galligaskins. Shoes were decorated with shoe roses.

5-C2   C. 1630s

During the Cavalier Period the silhouette is tubular and vertical in line. The doublet is high-waisted, with a skirt attached using laces. The collar is often called a falling band trimmed with lace, and the sleeves are full, slashed, and gathered into a cuff at the wrist. The breeches end below the knee and are worn with boots. The boot hose has a decorative cuff trimmed in lace that is folded over the top of the boot. Gauntlets (gloves with a wide cuff) and walking sticks are common accessories.

5-C3   C. 1640

The skirt on the doublet becomes longer and is sewn to the upper bodice without laces, and the waistline is closer to the natural waist. He is sporting a Van Dyck beard and mustache combination.

5-C5

5-C6

5-C4

5-C7

5-C8

5-C4   C. 1634

This is a variation on the doublet without a waist seam and an open front that is tied with a series of bows displaying the shirt underneath. He is holding a cape and a wide brim, low-crown hat with feathers, which was common for Cavaliers. Long curly hair with a love lock on one side tied in a ribbon was popular.

5-C5   C. 1632

Closeup image showing a very simple linen collar, more fitted sleeves, and a steeple-crown hat. The Puritans at this time had stricter codes for dress and rejected the overly decorated garments worn by the Cavaliers.

5-C6   C. 1632

Closeup image of a linen collar trimmed in lace, and a Van Dyck beard and mustache.

5-C7   C. EARLY 17TH CENTURY

A pair of gauntlets, which were a standard accessory for men, and used for fencing.

5-C8   C. 17TH CENTURY

A Cavalier hat with feathers.

5-C9   **5-C10**   **5-C11**

5-C9   C. 1642
As we near mid-century, the men's doublet is less fitted and worn open in the front with a sash around the high waistline. The sleeves are no longer sporting slashes and the collars are circular and simpler in decoration.

5-C10   C. 1673
In the middle part of the century, the doublet is a short open jacket with sleeves that reached the mid-forearm. A square linen collar was worn over this. The shirt is visible as it blouses over the breeches and extends beyond the sleeves to the wrist. The breeches, called petticoat breeches, are so full that they appear to be a divided skirt. Men wear hose with ribbons around the knee (garters) and shoes with bows. He is wearing a very tall steeple-crown hat.

5-C11   C. 1680
In the latter part of the century the style is more fitted. In this image the man is wearing a cape over a jacket and shirt with a jabot (a pleated lace collar). The breeches are tapered to just below the knee. The shoes in this image have a 2" red heel.

5-C12   C. LATE 17TH CENTURY
In this image we can see the early origins of the three-piece suit, which consists of a coat, waistcoat, and breeches worn over a shirt with a jabot at the neck. The coat is fitted to the waist with a full skirt on the lower half. The sleeves are straight and fitted with a wide cuff slightly above the wrist. Underneath is a sleeveless waistcoat that buttons to the knee. The breeches are tapered and to the knee. A long wide sash (baldric) is worn over the right shoulder to support the sword.

5-C12

5-C13

5-C14

5-C15

5-C16

5-C13   C. 1662

This is a closeup image of a steeple-crown hat and simple linen collar. We often see this image associated with the Puritan style of dress.

5-C14   C. LATE 17TH CENTURY

The long curly hair on this gentleman is presumed to be a wig in a natural color, which becomes popular at the end of the century. He is also wearing a Cavalier hat trimmed in feathers and a pleated lace jabot.

5-C15 & 5-C16   C. LATE 17TH CENTURY

These two images show the style of men's shoes worn in the latter half of the century. The bows and ribbons common in the early part of the century give way to buckles. The heel was usually 2" in height and the color was often red.

5-C17   5-C18

5-C17   C. 1633

By the 1630s, women's fashion was evolving from the structured style of the Late Renaissance to a more natural silhouette. The short-waisted bodice has tabs (basques) reminiscent of a man's doublet, and is worn with a stomacher covered with a sheer fichu trimmed in lace that ends with ribbon loops at the high waist. A narrow girdle is tied at the waist and finished with a rosette. The sleeves are full and trimmed in a lace edge ending at the elbow. The skirt is moderately full and split in the center front. She is wearing a falling ruff and wide-brimmed hat similar to the men.

5-C18   C. MID 17TH CENTURY

By mid century the waistline dips below the natural waist. The neckline was wide and off the shoulder. The décolletage was covered by the ruffled lace edge of the chemise. The sleeves, which end above the wrist, consist of two panes of fabric between puffs of fabric from the chemise, and edged in lace. The overskirt was shorter and revealed more of the petticoat, in contrasting fabric. The hair was parted in the middle with curls over the ears while back of hair was pulled up into a bun adorned with jewels.

5-C19   C. 1660

Spain continued to favor the fashion of the previous century and was slow to adopt the fashions of the other countries in Europe. In this image the young girl is wearing a farthingale of wide proportions. In a similar to fashion to 5-C18, there is an overskirt that is short and frames the skirt. The bodice is form-fitting and heavily corseted.

5-C19

5-C20

5-C21

5-C20   C. 1610

In the early part of the century women still wore ruffs. This style is called a millstone ruff, which had compact folds. The steeple-crown hat borrowed from men's fashions was worn over a Dutch cap.

5-C21   C. 1625

Women generally wore hats only for travelling or riding. The hats were similar to men's hats of the time such as this Cavalier hat, wide-brimmed and with feathers.

5-C22

5-C23

5-C24

5-C22   C. 1635

In Spain, the mantilla comes into fashion, which is a lace headscarf worn loosely over the hair.

5-C23   C. 1662

Headscarves made of linen worn over large circular collars are popular in Dutch fashion.

5-C24   C. 1641

One of the collar variations is this open-standing collar that covered the shoulders and was usually trimmed in lace.

5-C25   C. 1641

The Bertha collar, which can be seen on this woman, was a folded square of fabric trimmed in lace to form two layers. This was worn around the neck and shoulders.

5-C25

5-C26

5-C27

5-C26   C. 1653

This woman wears a circular linen collar, and a simple cap to cover her hair in back, which is popular with the Puritan style.

5-C27   C. 1660

The bodice and skirt are joined together with the point of the bodice overlapping the skirt. The bodice is fitted and fastened in front with stomacher. The neckline of the bodice is finished with a sheer capelet. The petticoat fell to the floor and the overskirt is gathered and pulled up in the back to create the soft draped fullness. The curls of hair at the side fall to the shoulder while the back of hair continues to be pulled up into a bun. She carries a feathered fan.

5-C28

5-C29

5-C28   C. 1660

Women's bodices are longer and dip lower in front. The skirts are longer than floor length in the front and train slightly in the back. The neckline is off the shoulder and finished with a sheer scarf that secures in the front of the bodice. Hair is more natural but still features the curls on the side of the hair and the bun in the back.

5-C30

5-C29   C. 1667

Later in the decade the bodice sits at the natural waist with a slight dip in the front. The sleeves are elbow-length, gathered in layers and finished with multiple layers of lace. The overskirt was split in center and revealed the contrasting petticoat. Hair was styled with curls and pulled up in the back.

5-C30   C. LATE 17TH CENTURY

In the latter part of the century, the silhouette is more vertical and slim. The underskirt is narrower and composed of a series of ruffled layers. The overskirt is pulled up in the back, creating a bustle effect, trimmed in ruffles, with a train. The bodice has a square neckline, and has a ruffled peplum in the back. Muffs made from fur and satin, and trimmed in bows, were a popular accessory.

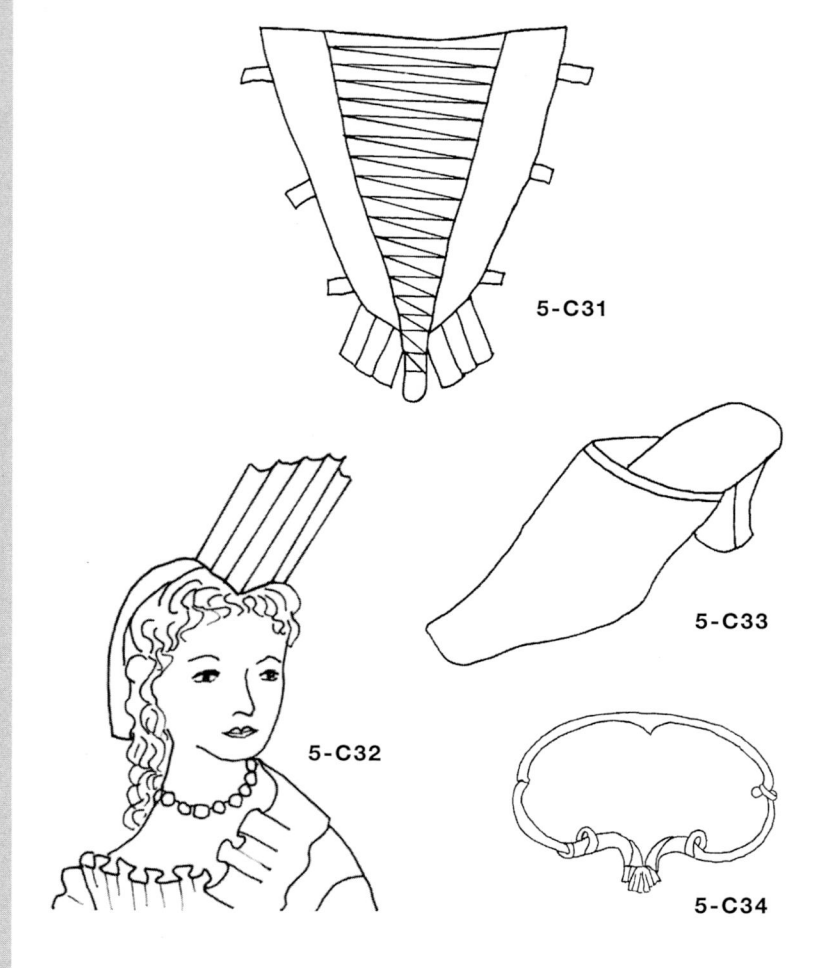

5-C31

5-C33

5-C32

5-C34

5-C31   C. 17TH CENTURY
A view of the stomacher with tabs used to attach to the bodice and laces used to tighten and constrict. Stomachers were embroidered or richly decorated with jewels, and stiffened with a removable busk in the front, made of metal, ivory, or wood.

5-C32   C. LATE 17TH CENTURY
The fontange is a headpiece created by a white linen cap coupled with a series of ruffles added in front and held in place with wire supports (commode).

5-C33   C. 1660–75
Backless shoes with heels (mules) were one of the shoe styles popular with women. The shoes were often made of brocade fabric or decorated leather.

5-C34   C. 1690
This is one example of a fan, a necessary accessory for women in social gatherings.

18th Century

The 18th century was impacted by the development of the Rococo style, the fascination with the Classical Roman Empire through the unearthing of Pompeii, and the beginnings of the Industrial Revolution in Europe. The Industrial Revolution helped to create a nouveau riche and middle class element in society. All of these elements affected style and its development during this time period. France dominated the culture in Western Europe and set the style in fashion, literature, and the decorative arts.

Architecture/Furniture/Décor

The scale and nature of various design choices at this time became reduced in size and suggested more of the intimate, rather than pomp and circumstance relationship with the surroundings. Classical style was still of interest, and more closely associated with the elements of the ancient culture. Follies and gardens, built around romantic ruins, became popular. Although Rococo style, with its asymmetrical elements of nature, created a feeling of light whimsy, this would be surpassed by Neoclassical designs reflected in both décor and furniture. Because of a growing middle class, furniture makers found that a whole new market had developed rather than just the aristocracy.

Costume

The Industrial Revolution brings about the invention of the Flying Shuttle, Spinning Jenny, and Spinning Machine during this century. These inventions increased the speed at which cotton fabric was made, which lowered costs and contributed to cotton becoming widely used in clothing. The clothing industry became more extensive with a diverse number of occupations such as linen drapers, dressmakers, tailors, and glovers. During this century, often referred to as the Georgian period, fashion and hairstyles go to the extremes, and reach their peak during the 1770s. Powdered wigs, lace ruffles, and excessive decoration and design on clothing were popular with both men and women. Cartoons, actual garments, and paintings provide much of the research.

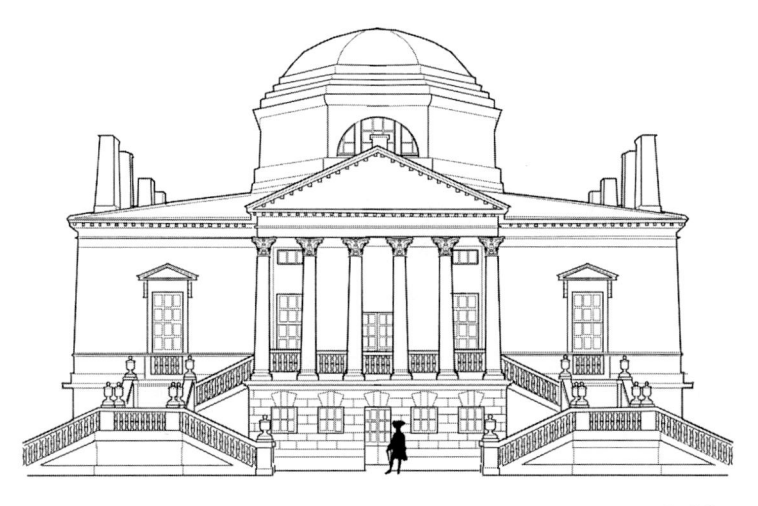

6-A1

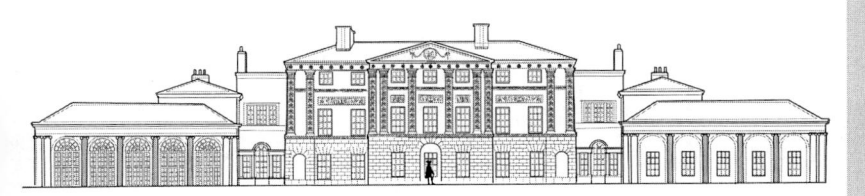

6-A2

6-A1 CHISWICK HOUSE

Chiswick House in London was designed by Lord Burlington in the Neo-Palladian style, giving the appearance of a Roman Villa. Built of brick and Portland stone with some stucco, it is a half cube with a central hall and rooms off of a central access. It was influenced by a number of Renaissance and Classical structures. Built in 1729.

6-A2 KENWOOD HOUSE

Kenwood House, London, located in Hampstead Heath, was remodeled by Robert Adam in a Neoclassical style. It was originally a red brick structure, but became stuccoed in a monochromatic color scheme. The subtle low relief of the classical elements in the pilasters and the surface of the walls are part of Adam's styles. 1779.

6-A3

6-A4

6-A3 TEMPLE OF PHILOSOPHY

Based in part on English garden design, the Temple of Philosophy at Ermenonville, France, was never meant to be finished but instead was created to look like a classical ruin. Structures such as these are usually located in a garden with plants that are meant to support the classical ruins look. 1770.

6-A4 PALLADIAN BRIDGE

Stowe Palladian Bridge in Wilton, England, was designed by Lord Pembroke, and is located in the estate gardens. Although created in the Palladian style, it is not based on an original Palladian structure. 1737.

6-A5

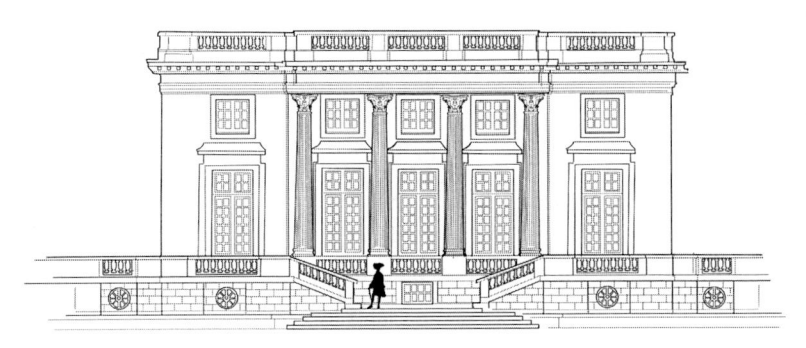

6-A6

6-A5   AMALIENBURG HUNTING LODGE

The Amalienburg Hunting Lodge is located on the grounds of the Nymphenburg Palace in Munich, Germany. The structure is in the Rococo style, constructed by François de Cuvilliés. In the central niche is a relief depicting a scene of Diana, goddess of the hunt. The pastel, two-color façade accentuates the Neoclassical and Rococo elements. 1739.

6-A6   PETIT TRIANON

The Petit Trianon, on the grounds of the Palace of Versailles, France, was designed by Ange-Jacques Gabriel for Louis XV's mistress, Madame de Pompadour, in the Neoclassical style. This view looks onto the gardens. The ground plan is based on a cube with each side relating to the view it faced. Meant to be an escape from the rigors of court life, it was also used by Marie Antoinette. 1768.

6.-D1

6-D2

6-D1 HALL OF MIRRORS, AMALIENBURG

The interior of the Amalienburg on the grounds of the
Nymphenburg Palace, particularly the Hall of Mirrors, is in the
Rococo style. Designed by Johann Baptist Zimmermann and
Joachim Dietrich, it contains the colors of silver and blue. The
mirrors are intended to reflect the elements of nature as seen
through the windows. 1739.

6-D2 INTERIOR AND SECRETARY DESIGN

This drawing is taken from an etching by the artist Franz Xavier
Habermann of a design of an interior and secretary in the Rococo
style. The tall cabinet has a clock at the top and pedestals on
either side. The use of nature and putti in an asymmetrical way is
in keeping with the Rococo style. 1770.

6-D3

6-D4

6-D3 DINING ROOM OF THE PETIT TRIANON
Architectural details found in the dining room of the Petit Trianon
on the grounds of Versailles are in the Louis XVI style. The
Neoclassical elements such as crossed torches, ribbons, and
swags of roses, coupled with light pastel colors, comprise this
style. Late 18th century.

6-D4 ENTRY HALL AT SYON HOUSE
The Entry Hall at Syon House, London was designed by Robert
Adam in the Neoclassical style. Adam incorporated Classical
motifs such as coffered ceilings, triglyphs in the lower level
cornice, Classical columns and Classical statues. The room is
accentuated in pastel colors and soft whites. 1778.

6-F1

6-F2

6-F3

6-F4

6-F5

6-F1   EARLY GEORGIAN CHAIR

This chair can be considered either Early Georgian or Queen Anne as it contains elements that are found in both styles, such as cabriole legs with a scallop shell on the knees, ball and claw feet, and stretchers connecting the legs. Early 18th century.

6-F2   CHIPPENDALE SIDE CHAIR

This Chippendale chair has cabriole legs with acanthus leaf images on knees and on the pierced splat, with scrolls and scroll feet. Mid 18th century.

6-F3   CHIPPENDALE ARMCHAIR

This Chippendale armchair has a pierced splat, cabriole legs, ball and claw feet, and shepherd's crook arms. Upholstery covers the seat support and is secured with brass tacks. Mid 18th century.

6-F4   CHIPPENDALE COMMODE

This half-round Chippendale commode is in the Classical style, with marquetry on all surfaces using Classical elements, with doors on the front. 1778.

6-F5   GEORGE HEPPLEWHITE SIDEBOARD

This sideboard, designed by George Hepplewhite, has a bowed front with subtle marquetry on the fan designs on the door corners. Late 18th century.

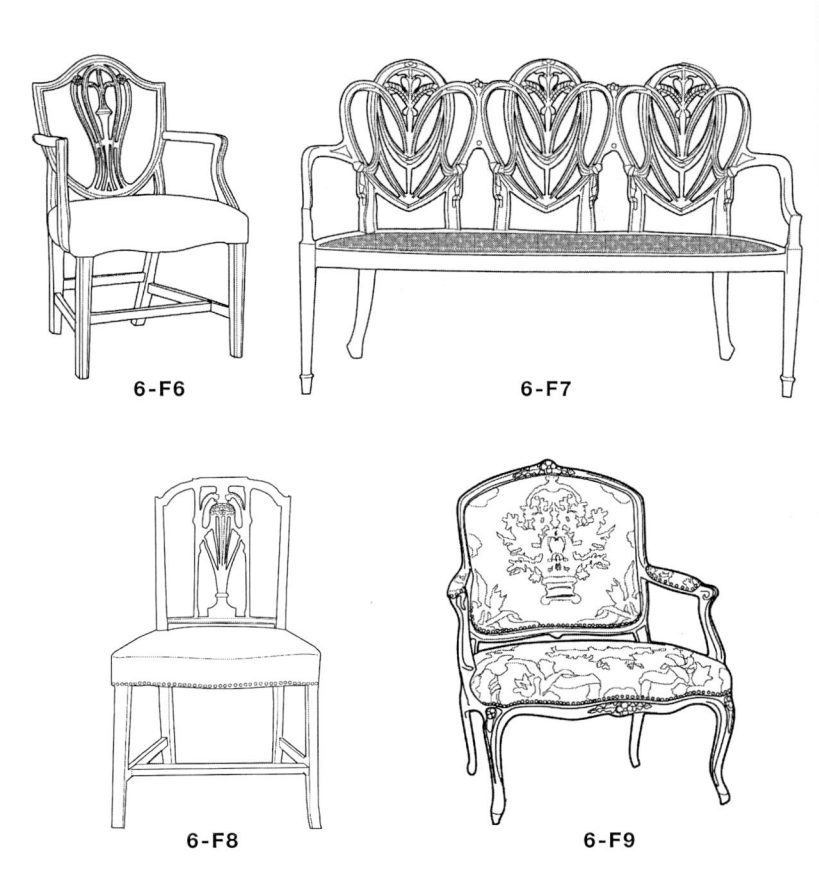

6-F6

6-F7

6-F8

6-F9

6-F6   HEPPLEWHITE ARMCHAIR

This shield back armchair, designed by George Hepplewhite, is referred to as an elbow chair because of the short setback to the armrests which helps to accommodate jacket peplums and skirts. Seats typically have a bow front. Late 18th century.

6-F7   SHIELD BACK SETTEE

This settee, designed by George Hepplewhite, has a shield back with draped scarf pattern on the pierced back. The seat is caned with sloped armrests. Late 18th century.

6-F8   SHERATON SIDE CHAIR

This side chair is designed by Thomas Sheraton. Its pierced back splat has a Classical urn shape, and the narrow front legs turn out slightly at the very bottom. Late 18th century.

6-F9   LOUIS XV ARMCHAIR

This armchair is in the Louis XV style with a gray lacquer frame and violet patterned covering. It was one of a collection of pieces designed and constructed for the Château de Talcy, French. Mid 18th century.

6-F10

6-F11

6-F12

6-F13

6-F10   LA DUCHESSE DAYBED
This daybed is in the Louis XV style, with gilded cabriole legs and an embroidered silk covering. Mid 18th century.

6-F11   BOMBE FRONT COMMODE
This commode is in the Louis XV style with a bombe front, cabriole legs, gilded brass mounts, and subtle marquetry. The top is made of Rosso levanto marble. 1740.

6-F12   SMALL WRITING DESK
This small writing desk is in the Louis XV style, created by Martin Carlin, and includes inset porcelain plaques, gilded brass mounts, and elongated cabriole legs.1768.

6-F13   LOUIS XVI ARMCHAIR
The armchair is in the Louis XVI style and contains Classical images of the acanthus leaf and fluting on the legs. The embroidery contains romantic images and is held in place by decorative tacks. Late 18th century.

6-F14

6-F15

6-F16

6-F17

6-F14 SMALL SOFA, SETTEE

This small settee is in the Louis XVI style, with floral and pastoral subject matter embroidered into the upholstery fabric. Classical elements are incorporated into the design of the frame, and can also be found on the twisted fluting on the legs. Late 18th century.

6-F15 WRITING TABLE

Small writing table in the Louis XVI style, with gold-plated brass mounts and a pierced metal retaining fence around the desktop. Late 18th century.

6-F16 DIRECTOIRE ARMCHAIR

This armchair is in the Directoire/transitional style which includes scroll back and lion heads on the armrests, as well as spindle legs with Classical elements such as acanthus leaves and twisted fluting from the Louis XVI style. 1790.

6-F17 EMPIRE LOUNGE

This Neoclassical style lounge and oil lamp are taken from a painting by Jacques-Louis David. The lounge and lamp are in the Empire style with Classical elements such as reverse scrolls on either end of the lounge and tube pillows and rosettes. 1800.

6-C1

6-C2

6-C1   C. EARLY 18TH CENTURY

In the early part of the century, styles are similar to the late 17th century. The flared coat falls slightly below the knee. The sleeves are longer with wide cuffs revealing the lower edge of shirt. The waistcoat is slightly shorter than the coat and buttons all the way down. The knee breeches are buttoned or buckled just below the knee. The jabot, baldric, and walking stick from the previous century are still in vogue. Shoes traditionally have a 2" heel and are often decorated with bows.

6-C2   C. 1740

The coat is still flared with pleating in the back but the pockets on the coat and waistcoat are placed higher at hipline. The waistcoat buttons only to the waist. The simple cravat combined with a stock tied at the neck is popular. The shoe heels are shorter and the bows are replaced by buckles. The wig style includes a periwig with a braid or pony tail in the back tied in a ribbon.

6-C3

6-C4

6-C5

6-C3 C. 1750

During the mid-century, the coat is slimmer with less pleating in the back, neckline is higher and has a turnover collar. The sleeves are wrist length, and tapered with narrow cuffs. The waistcoat is shorter and buttons higher on the neck. Breeches are more fitted.

6-C4 C. EARLY 18TH CENTURY

Wigs were full and curly until 1730s. They could be powdered white or a natural hair color.

6-C5 C. 1740

In the mid-century, wig styles were shoulder length and less exaggerated than previous decades.

6-C6

6-C7

6-C8

6-C6   C. MID 18TH CENTURY

The tricorne hat is the predominant hat until the last quarter of the century.

6-C7   C. 1769

Coat is less full and has a small turnover collar. The waistcoat length is shorter and sits at the lower hipline. Waistcoats often had lapels, similar to modern vests. Breeches are more fitted and button at knee for a tighter fit.

6-C8   C. 1772

Coat with turnover collar buttons to below waist. Cravat, walking stick, tricorne, and periwig are still fashionable in the early 1770s.

6-C9

6-C10

6-C9 C. 1777

As the decade progresses, the jacket becomes slimmer, cut-away in the front, and slopes to the back. The back is tailored without pleats. The waistcoat is now shorter and closer to the modern length of the vest. Breeches are very fitted.

6-C10 C. 1789

The French Revolution brought about a trend for "Sans Culottes," meaning without knee breeches. These were loose trousers that were ankle length and referred to as pantaloons. The jackets were loose. Waistcoat is double-breasted with large lapels. In this image, he is wearing wooden clogs decorated with a flower. The bicorne hat comes into fashion. The colors of red, white, and blue, the colors of liberty, were popular.

6-C12

6-C11

6-C13

6-C11 C.1796

An "Incroyable" is the "beatnik" of the 18th century. Long-skirted coats with extremely wide lapels, and tight knee breeches tied at the knee were the fashion. A long cravat was tied high around the neck. The hair was naturally long and disheveled, and they wore a bicorne or silk top hat.

6-C12 C. 1790

The greatcoat came into popularity. It was double-breasted with a full skirt and had an attached cape. This was worn as an overcoat and in military wear.

6-C13 C. 1760

This is a closeup view of breeches showing the button flap front and lacing in the back.

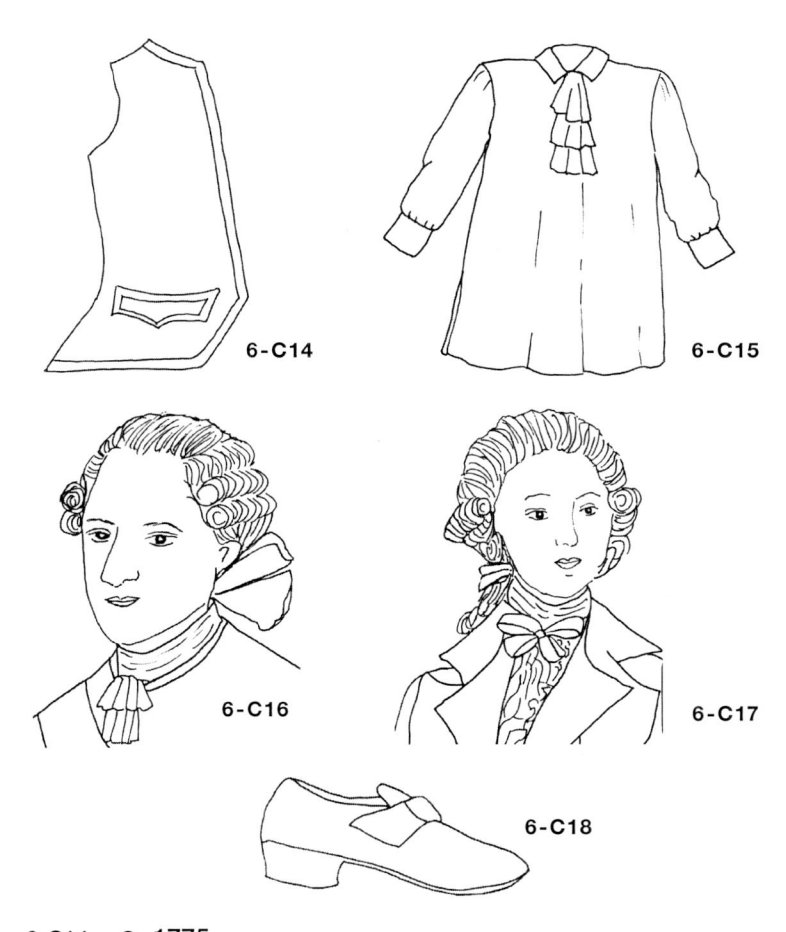

6-C14

6-C15

6-C16

6-C17

6-C18

6-C14   C. 1775

A side view of the waistcoat from the latter part of the century. This style had a square bottom and sat just below the waist.

6-C15   C. 1775

The shirt has a turnover collar and ruffled front. Sleeves are slimmer than in previous century and had cuffs.

6-C16   C. 1773

The wig shown here has two rolls of curls on the side and hair is gathered in back of head and decorated with a wide bow. The wigs can be powdered or natural color. The gentleman in this image is wearing a stock around his neck with a ruffled shirt.

6-C17   C. 1781

In this image the hairstyle is a bit fuller on top with one set of curls and still tied in back. The stock worn around his neck is finished by tying a bow in the front. The coat has wide lapels.

6-C18   C. MID TO LATE 18TH CENTURY

The side view of a man's shoe showing the moderate heel, small tongue, and simple buckle.

6-C19

6-C20

6-C19   C.1720

This style of dress is known as a robe à la française or sack-back gown, and sometimes referred to as a Watteau back gown, named after the painter. The back of the gown is full and pleats into a narrow yoke, high on the neck. The front of the dress hung loosely from the shoulder to floor. In the early part of the century, it was worn as casual wear and also maternity wear. Later in the century it was worn for formal occasions. (See 6-C24 and 6-C25)

6-C20   C. 1740

This wide mantua style gown was popular for a short period of time in the early 18th century. The width of the skirt was extreme and is supported by structures called panniers, often made of whalebone. Sleeves are elbow length with flounces. Fans continue to be popular accessories.

6-C22

6-C21

6-C21   C. 1745

Court gown and petticoat. The bodice is heavily boned and
has a square neck with lace trim and elbow-length sleeves with
flounces. The shape of the dress is elliptical with more fullness on
the sides and flatter silhouette front and back.

6-C22   C. 1759

Madame Pompadour had considerable influence in fashion mid-
century. The bodices were heavily boned and extended to a point
in front and were decorated with bows, flowers, and lace. The
sleeves were elbow-length, finished with a double row of ruffles
or lace. The skirt was split in the front revealing the petticoat.
The pompadour hairstyle consisted of hair pulled up in front,
and arranged in the back of the head with curls or twists and
decorated with ribbons, flowers, or pearls. A separate frilled
neckband, similar to a choker, was worn.

6-C24

6-C23

6-C23   C. 1763

The shawl-style dress was a simpler gown that was worn during the daytime and for less formal occasions. The skirt of the petticoat had less width than the more ornate ball gowns. The overgown was shorter and pulled up in the back. A shawl was worn around the shoulders.

6-C24 & 6-C25   C. 1765–1775

The sack-back gown (robe à la française) in this image is the more formal version of the earlier style seen in 6-C19. It consisted of a bodice with a square neckline and elbow-length sleeves, and a skirt and petticoat supported by panniers. In the second image, the back of the dress is displayed. The neckline is lower but still has the traditional box pleats.

6-C25

6-C26

6-C26   C. 1770S

In the 1770s, ladies' court gowns reach extremes, which is
complimented by the extremes in hairstyles during the same
period. The skirt has a series of swags of gauze on the lower edge
which is sometimes referred to as the wedding cake style. The
bodice is low cut and square and the point in the front dips below
the waist. The sleeves have multiple puffs of fabric trimmed in lace.

6-C27

6-C28

6-C27　C. 1770S

The polonaise gown is named after a popular dance at the time. The petticoat is ankle-length with the overskirt of the gown pulled up in the back using draw cords and ribbons, creating several swags in the back of the dress. The bodice has elbow-length sleeves and a collar of lace around the neckline of the dress.

6-C28　C. 1770S

The servant dress is much simpler and not as wide as the court dresses. She is wearing a fichu that crosses in front of the bodice and ties in the back, an apron, and simple mob cap (gathered linen cap with flounce). Aprons were popular with women of all classes as a form of fashion.

6-C29

6-C30

6-C29   C. 1776

This is an example of a riding costume for women, called a redingote. It was adapted from the red coat uniforms worn by British soldiers fighting in America. The jacket was long and tailored, with a turnover collar and lapels. The sleeves are simple and fitted with a small cuff.

6-C30   C. 1783

In the 1780s, dresses lose their fullness and panniers and the silhouette shifts to more fullness at the back of the dress. The neckline on the bodice is still square, and adorned with ruffles, and sleeves are full at top and more fitted to the wrist. This outfit would be worn during daytime.

6-C31

6-C32

6-C33

6-C31   C. 1758

This is an example of an early pompadour hairstyle. The height is moderate with curls in the back. The hairstyle could be dressed with bows, ribbons, and jewels.

6-C32   C. 1765

The pompadour hairstyle becomes higher in the front with curls at the top and longer curls down the back.

6-C33   C. 1774

Along with the extremes in dress, the coiffures were higher, larger, and ornately adorned. Brimmed hats perched on the top of the hair were tied under the neck.

6-C35

6-C34

6-C36

6-C37

6-C34 & 6-C35   C. 1776

Hairstyles were often the basis of many cartoons of the time. The extremes in height were often supported by crinoline and padding. The coiffures were often powdered white. The woman in 6-C34 is wearing a frigate to honor a naval victory during the American Revolution. The hairstyle in 6-C35 is decorated with laurel leaves and feathers.

6-C36   C. 1780

Headwear had to adapt to the extremes of hairstyles. In this image we see a mob cap perched on top of the hair, and the hood of a cape over both.

6-C37   C. MID TO LATE 18TH CENTURY

Low-crown, wide-brimmed hats, dressed with feathers and flowers, were popular for daywear. They sometimes had a ribbon that tied under the neck in a bow.

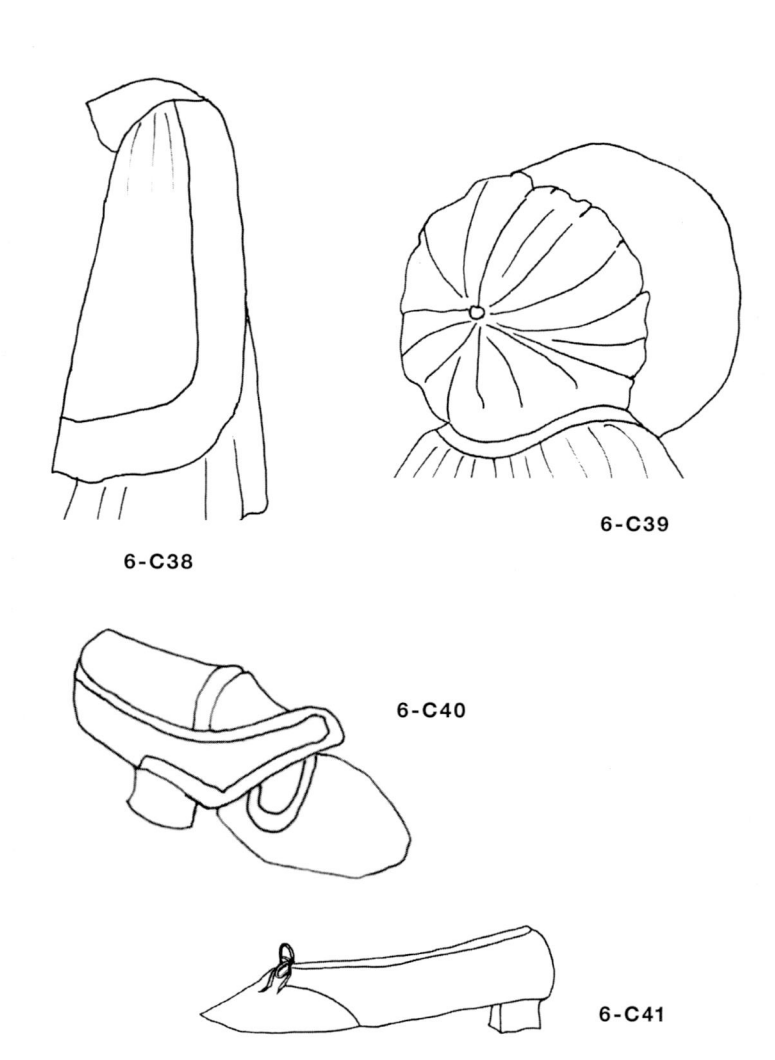

6-C38

6-C39

6-C40

6-C41

6-C38 & 6-C39 C. MID 18TH CENTURY

Capes with matching hoods were popular throughout the century. The second image is an expanded view of the hood.

6-C40 C. 1760S

The shoes were usually made of brocade, with a thicker heel, and a buckle that curved around the instep of the shoe. By mid-century the toes were rounded, instead of pointed. The silhouette is very similar to the men's styles of footwear.

6-C41 C. 1790

At the end of the century we see the slipper replace the heeled shoe in popularity.

Early 19th Century

The Industrial Revolution accelerates during this century because of steam as a power source, and this has a serious impact on architecture, furniture, and clothing, as goods are mass produced at lower cost. The middle class grows and establishes an important place in society, and many workers move from rural areas to the cities to work in the factories. Although this time period begins, as the previous period ends, with a desire for Neoclassical styles, this will eventually give way to the revival of various previous styles.

Architecture / Furniture / Décor

Neoclassical styles such as Adam and Jefferson are popular at the beginning of this time period, but eventually start to include Egyptian, Greek, and Gothic revivals as well. While most government buildings in America will maintain the Neoclassical style as a statement of power, many universities and museums will desire the Gothic Revival style which relates to older institutions in Europe. Domestic structures in Europe will use a range of styles from Gothic Revival to Greek Revival, but in America many domestic styles will still relate to the previously established styles of the Colonial era. Much like architecture, furniture and décor will either be coordinated with the general style of the structure, or may be one of these revival styles. In America, a simplistic style created by the Shaker community will also be popular, placing function over any type of decoration.

Costume

It is during this time that Paris is established as the center of fashion, and maintains that designation even today. The clothing of the Regency period, especially for women, harkens back to the classical Greek silhouette. The women go to great lengths to emulate the ancient statues by wearing sheer muslin dresses that hug and drape across the body. The male silhouette has a more natural line as well. Pantaloons eventually transition into long pants, and the beginnings of the modern three-piece suit are seen. The Romantic period again moves to extremes in width of shoulders and sleeves for both men and women, while emphasizing small waists. Even men were known to wear corsets during this time. Information about style is found in actual garments, paintings, and fashion periodicals that have been preserved and reprinted.

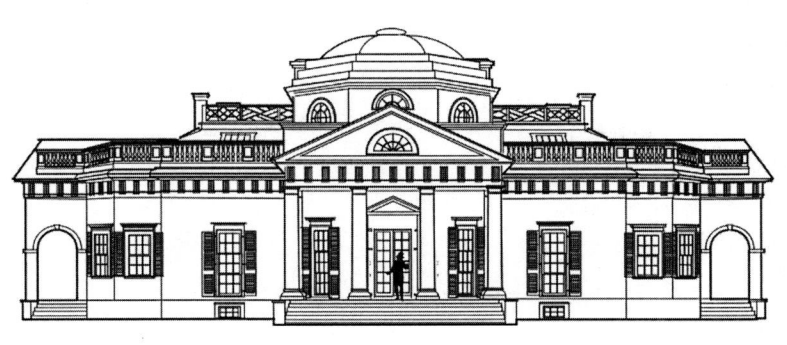

7-A1

7-A2

7-A1 MONTICELLO

Monticello, designed by Thomas Jefferson, is considered in the Jefferson Style, which includes red brick, white trim, Etruscan columns, and Palladian elements such as the white railing above the cornice. Virginia. 1806.

7-A2 OTIS HOUSE

Federal or Adam Style, constructed for Harrison Gray Otis in Boston. Adam style consists of red brick and white trim, double-hung windows, iron railings, a Palladian window on the second floor center, and a fan light over the front door. 1796.

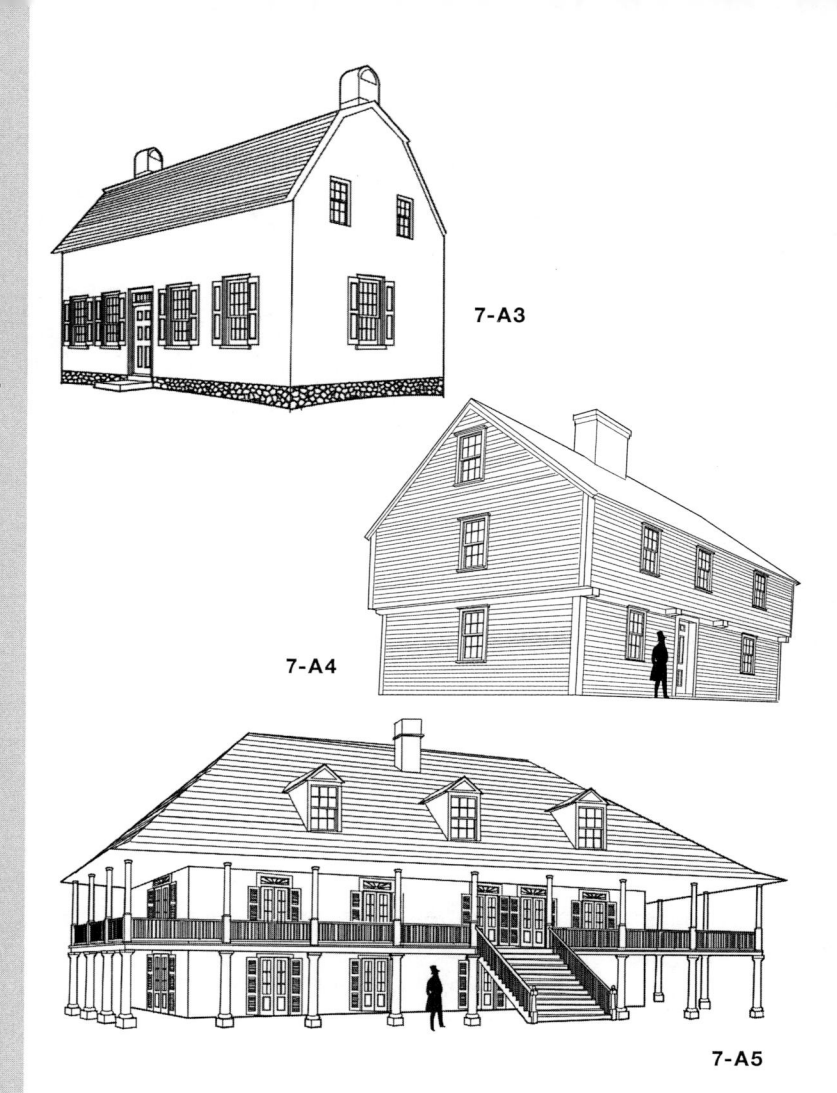

7-A3

7-A4

7-A5

7-A3 DUTCH COLONIAL

Dutch Colonial Style, Hudson River area, constructed of stone or brick, with gambrel roof. Late 18th to early 19th century.

7-A4 MCINTIRE HOUSE

McIntire House, Maine, in the English Garrison style, with characteristics including overhang of the second floor, double-hung windows, and clapboard siding. Although constructed in 1707, this house (along with 7-A5 and 7-A7) should be considered as an introduction to early 19th century American architecture.

7-A5 PARLANGE PLANTATION HOUSE

The Parlange Plantation House in Louisiana is in the French Colonial style. The ground floor is reserved for storage, servants' quarters, and kitchen. All floors above are for the family. 1754.

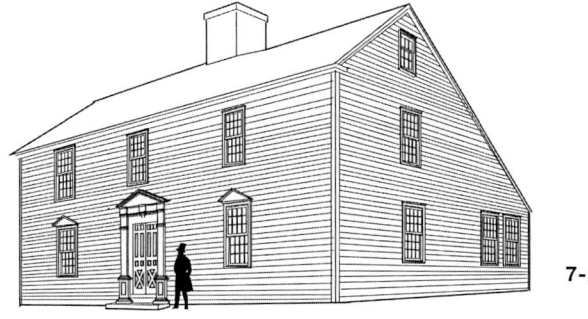

7-A6

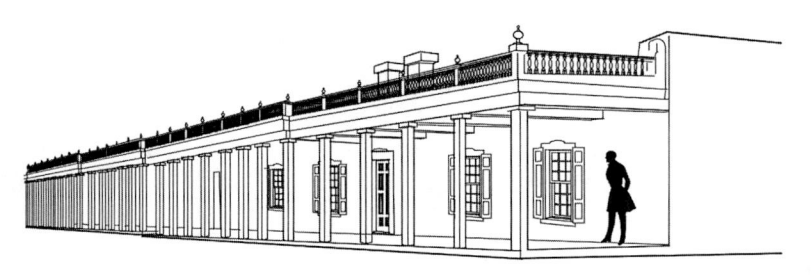

7-A7

7-A8

7-A6   SALTBOX STYLE COLONIAL

In this Saltbox Style Colonial House, located in Massachusetts, the back of the roof is longer than the front. Late 18th to early 19th century.

7-A7   PALACE OF THE GOVERNORS

The Palace of the Governors, located in New Mexico, is in the Spanish Colonial style, with adobe brick and a stucco coating, and a long veranda with flat roofs. 1790.

7-A8   ROSELAND COTTAGE

The Roseland Cottage in Connecticut is in the Gothic Revival style, with trim under the eave of the gable end, pointed arch windows, and steep roofs. 1846.

7-A9

7-A10

7-A9 TYLER HOUSE

Tyler House, Pennsylvania, in the Greek Revival style, has symmetrical design Classical columns with Ionic capitals and a portico with a pronounced cornice. 1840.

7-A10 ENTRANCE TO PUBLIC CEMETERY

This cemetery entrance, located in New Haven, Connecticut, is in the Egyptian Revival style, designed by Henry Austin. Elements include a broad base, cove cornice, and lotus-bundled columns. 1845.

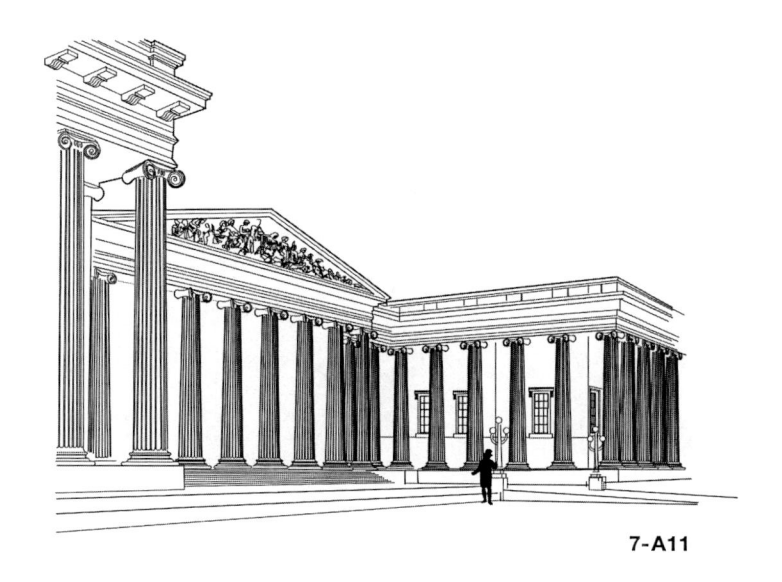

7-A11

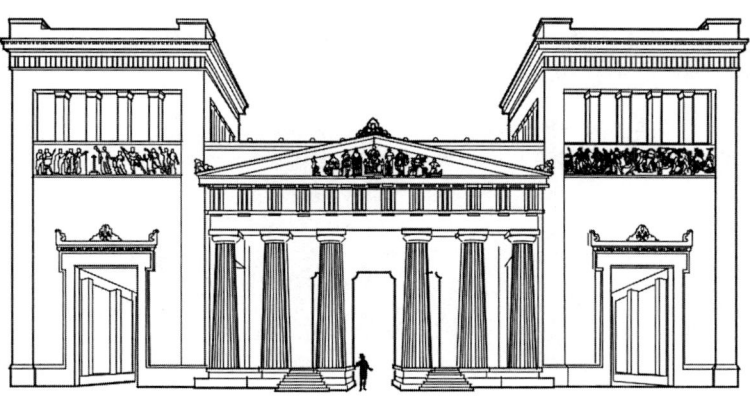

7-A12

7-A11   BRITISH MUSEUM

The British Museum, located in London, is in the Greek Revival style, designed by Sir Robert Smirke. The characteristics of the Greek Revival style in this structure are a center pillared portico, Ionic columns, and a pronounced cornice. 1825–1850.

7-A12   PROPYLAEA

The Propylaea located in Munich, Germany is in the Greek Revival style, designed by Leo von Klenze. Elements include Doric columns, a pillared portico, and aedicule door trim. Designed in 1848, but not constructed until 1862.

7-D1

7-D2

7-D1   FEDERAL STYLE INTERIOR

This interior is considered Neoclassical or American Federal style, with Classical elements such as columns, swagged drapes, and cove molding with Greco-Roman elements. 1780–1830.

7-D2   GREEK REVIVAL INTERIOR

This Greek Revival parlor in New York was designed by Duncan Phyfe. The style consists of a heavy cornice and pilasters on the doorframe, with Greek shouldered architrave trim and wave motif on the header above the door. 1825–1837.

7-D3   REFORM CLUB

The Reform Club in London is in the Neoclassical style, designed by Charles Barry. Elements include Ionic and Corinthian capitals, Roman-influenced cornices, and coffered archways. 1841.

7-D3

7-D4

7-D4   STRAWBERRY HILL HOUSE GALLERY

The Strawberry Hill House Gallery, London, is in the Gothic Revival
style, designed by Thomas Pitt. Gothic elements are the fan vault
ceilings, pointed arches, niches with a quatrefoil pattern, finials,
and scalloping. Introduced in the late 18th century, Gothic Revival
style was prevalent throughout the 19th century. 1776.

7-D5

7-D5   EGYPTIAN REVIVAL

This interior is in the Egyptian Revival style, designed by Thomas Hope. The design includes hieroglyphics in the frieze area and furniture in the Egyptian vein. 1807.

7-F1

7-F2

7-F3

7-F4

7-F1 FEDERAL SIDE CHAIR

This side chair is in the Federal style and was created by Samuel McIntire in Massachusetts. The shield back has an urn and swagged fabric created by piercing through the back with a low-relief design. The straight front legs have inlay patterns on them, spade-shaped feet, and a bow front to the seat. 1794–1799.

7-F2 LADDERBACK SIDE CHAIR

This Shaker-style ladderback side chair is in light wood with a woven reed seat. The back is tall and other than the elliptical-turned spindle tops, the chair is devoid of decoration. 1840.

7-F3 GOTHIC REVIVAL HALL CHAIR

This hall chair is in the Gothic Revival style with birdcage pierced legs, tall back with extended pinnacled tops, and pendant trefoil decoration under the seat rails. 1850.

7-F4 SHERATON ARMCHAIR

The Thomas Sheraton armchair has Neoclassical elements such as the curved chair back with the double X. The chair also has the classic Sheraton arms which turn down at the front toward the seat. It is a painted chair with Neoclassical elements incorporated into the design. The seat is caned. 1800.

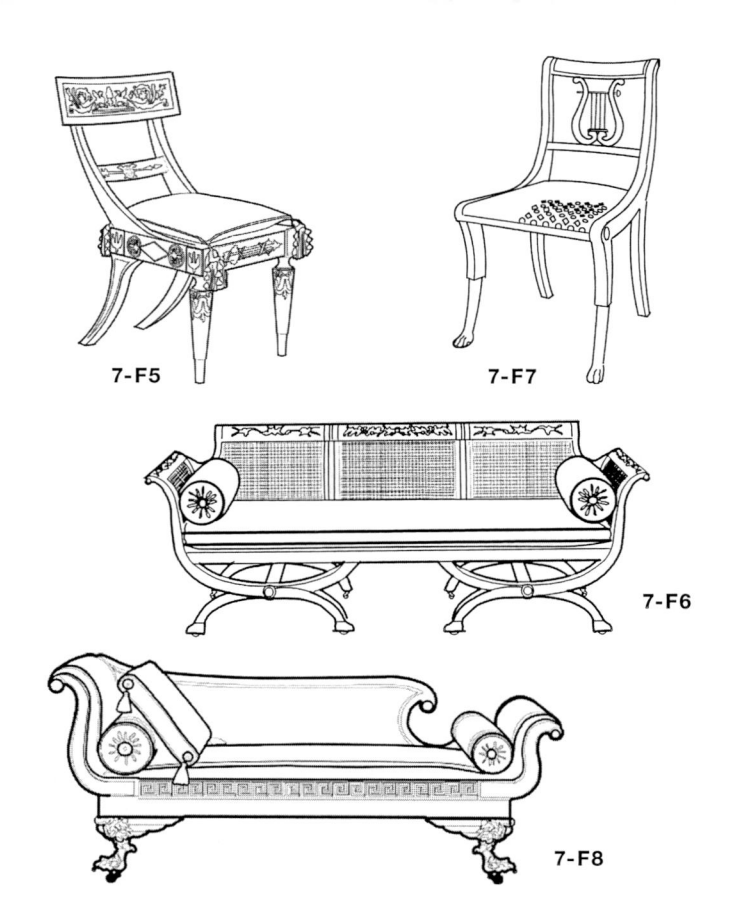

7-F5

7-F7

7-F6

7-F8

7-F5 GREEK REVIVAL CHAIR

Greek Revival, tablet-back side chair, designed by John Latrobe and created by John and Hugh Finlay, Baltimore. It is in the klismos style with painted Greek details, referred to at the time as a "fancy chair" because of the painted details. 1815–1820.

7-F6 GREEK REVIVAL SETTEE

This Duncan Phyfe settee is in the Greek Revival style. The piece is made out of mahogany with caning on the back and seat. The X-shaped legs, taken from Classical folding chairs, are considered part of the Phyfe style. New York. 1810–1820.

7-F7 DUNCAN PHYFE SIDE CHAIR

This scroll-back side chair with lyre splat was designed by Duncan Phyfe. The saber front legs become animal legs with paws for feet halfway down the leg. All are considered part of Phyfe's style. New York. 1810–1820.

7-F8 DUNCAN PHYFE RÉCAMIER

This lounge, or Récamier sofa, in the Greek Revival style was designed by Duncan Phyfe. In addition to the reverse scroll arm rests, it has winged paw feet. 1815–1820.

7-C2

7-C1

7-C3

7-C1   C. 1800

The vertical silhouette dominates during the first part of the century. The double-breasted coat is cut slightly above the waist in front revealing the waistcoat below. Coat curves to back creating tails that fall to knee. The rolling collar sits high, and the sleeves are fitted with narrow cuffs at the wrist. The breeches have a button-up front flap and are fastened at the knees. Breeches were required at court until 1830. Cravat tied around neck and pleated shirt are worn with waistcoat that has a high standing collar. Shorter boots were worn with longer hose and breeches by conservatives at court.

7-C2   C. 1800

A closeup view of a cravat and coat collar. Cravat was bulky in the early part of century as it was made of cotton and wrapped twice around the neck and tied in a bow in front. The coat has a high rolling collar over lapels. A single-breasted waistcoat sits high on neck. The hair was medium length and worn in a casual wavy style with sideburns that extended to chin.

7-C3   C. 1801

Side view of the double-breasted tail coat showing the high rolled collar, cravat, and waistcoat which is double-breasted and has lapels.

7-C4

7-C5

7-C4   C. 1804

Side view of the tailcoat worn with trousers fitted below the knee and tall boots with cuffs, often referred to as wellingtons. This is an example of a riding costume.

7-C5   C. 1807

The tailcoat could be slimmer at the back of the coat and have split tails. The shirt has a standing collar that sits high on the face with the cravat wrapped around. The waistcoat collar can be seen extending over the rolled collar of the coat. The chain and fob on the watch, which was worn in the right pocket of the waistcoat, can be seen hanging below the coat. His breeches are very tight, a popular style with younger males, and have buttons at the lower part of leg. The tightness of the trousers required a knitted fabric, or leather, for comfort.

7-C6

7-C7

7-C6 C. 1812

The military attire was the inspiration for later styles such as the redingote. The jacket with the standing collar is cut high in the front revealing the baldric sash and the waistcoat that sits at the natural waistline. The epaulets and buttons finish off the jacket. The knee breeches are buttoned at the side, and the boots extend to the knee.

7-C7 C. 1812

Another depiction of the uniform showing off the single-breasted waistcoat with pockets, underneath the coat which is cut-away to tails in the back. The short hairstyle with bangs was another popular look for men in the early part of the century.

7-C8

7-C9

7-C8   C. 1815

By 1815, the collar sits lower on the coat and the tails are falling to a few inches above the knee. The waistcoat is not as high on the neck and the cravat has less bulk. The knee breeches worn with the shorter boots indicate that this is a court garment.

7-C9   C. 1825

By the 1820s the frock coat makes an entrance and is worn in the daytime as well as the tailcoat. The double-breasted coat has a seam at the waistline and a flared skirt. The notched collar is narrow in comparison to previous decade. The sleeves have more fullness at the top and are referred to as leg-of-mutton sleeves. The top hat becomes the norm for both daytime and evening/formal wear and continues throughout the century. The ankle-length trousers have a single front button closure with straps on the bottom which hook over the instep of shoes and boots. Gloves would have been worn by gentlemen for both daytime and evening.

7-C10   7-C11

7-C10   C. 1826

The tail coat evolves and has a narrow shawl collar and leg-of-mutton sleeves. The shoulder seam extends to beyond the natural shoulder line. The tail in the back is narrower and shorter than previous decade. A watch fob hangs below the waist in front. The hair is worn with more curls and the sideburns widen closer to the chin. This is referred to as mutton chops. The cravat becomes longer and wider, is pleated and folded and hides the front of the shirt. It could be black or other colors and prints, although white was worn for evening.

7-C11   C. 1826

This is an example of a greatcoat, which has a high standing stiff collar and a cape-collar over the shoulder. The length was generally at mid-calf. The trousers on this male are above the ankle bone which was a popular style with dandies during the 1820s.

7-C12

7-C13

7-C12   C. 1830

This front view of the frockcoat shows the emphasis on the small waist in contrast to the leg-of-mutton sleeves and wide flared skirt. Men were known to have corseted themselves to achieve the smaller waist between 1820 and 1850. The strap under the instep goes out of fashion in the 1830s.

7-C13   C. 1831

The silhouette of this gentleman shows a wide shoulder line, enhanced by the wide notched collar, sloping shoulders and narrow waist on the tailcoat. The cravat is wide and long, hides the shirt, and combined with the double-breasted laced waistcoat gives the chest emphasis which was a popular look. He wears spurs on his boots which could suggest riding attire.

7-C14

7-C15

7-C14   C. 1833

The tail coat has a shawl collar, and is fitted at the waist. Trousers were heavily pleated at the waist to accent the small waistline. The waistcoat opening sits lower by the chest and has a notched collar. Some gentlemen would wear two waistcoats together, and would often combine a print with a solid for contrast. Top coats continued to be worn in both daytime and evening until mid-century.

7-C15   C. 1833

The Garrick coat is an overcoat, similar in style to the greatcoat, and has a large deep collar and cape-collar. The Garrick could have up to five cape-collars in its design. The coat is very full, and has a tabbed closure at the waist.

7-C16 **7-C17**

7-C16 C. 1834

This top coat is sometimes referred to as a redingote, especially in France. It follows the line and silhouette of the frock coat but extends to below the calf.

7-C17 C. 1842

By the 1840s the silhouette is slimmer and natural. The waistline dips below the natural waist much like the silhouette in women's fashion at the same time. The cravat is narrow and tied with little bulk at the neck. The waistcoat is open lower on the chest revealing more of the shirt. He is wearing a tailcoat under the top coat. The hairstyle is curly and parts on the side, and the sideburns extend to the chin creating a narrow beard.

7-C19

7-C18

7-C20

7-C18   C. 1842

Side view of the coat which falls to just below the knee. The
ruffled shirt is visible and the neckline is finished with a cravat. The
sleeves are again fitted and no longer have the fullness at the top
of the sleeve.

7-C19   C. 1833

A closeup of the ruffled shirt and cravat. The hairstyle in this image
is sometimes referred to as a pompadour.

7-C20   C. 1830S

The top hat was a staple throughout the century. The color was
black or dark grey and they were made of silk or beaver. The height
and shape of the crown and the width and shape of the brim were
always changing. In this image, we see a bell topper, the distinction
being the wider top and narrower base. We often see this style in
illustrations of the Mad Hatter from *Alice in Wonderland*.

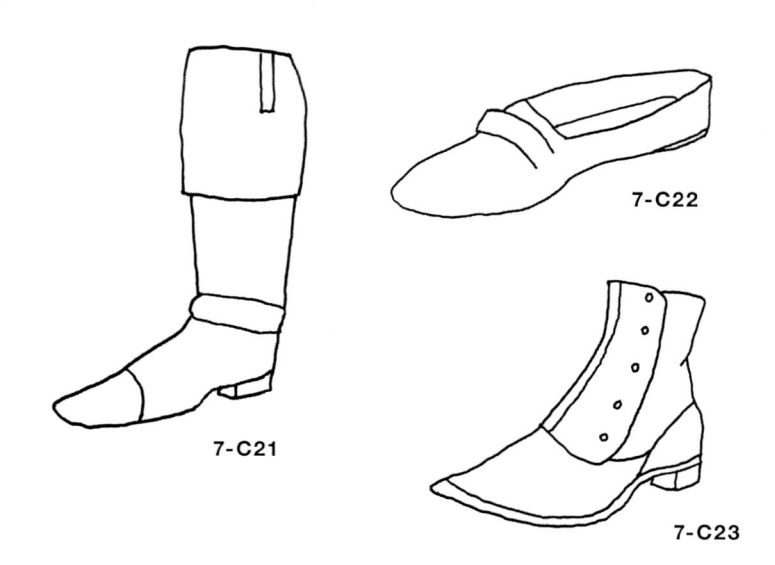

7-C21

7-C22

7-C23

7-C21 C. 1810–20

The tall boot is often referred to as a wellington style. It had narrow rounded toes, a cuff, and was cut away at the back of the knee.

7-C22 C. 1827

A man's dress shoe with oval toe, made of leather, with a narrow strap for a buckle. It resembles the slipper shoes worn by women at this time.

7-C23 C. 1840S

Square toe, five button dress boot popular in this decade for men.

7-C24 C. 1800

The silhouette for females at the beginning of the 19th century harkens back to the Classical Greek style once again. The overall line is vertical and slim with a high waistline and square neckline. The sleeves were short and gathered to a band. The preferred fabric was muslin and it draped softly around the figure to create the look of the ancient Greek statues. Very little jewelry was worn during this time. The hair was dressed in curls which framed the face and a chignon high on the back of the head. Simple slipper sandals were the fashion in the first half of the century.

7-C25 C. 1805

The evening dress followed similar lines but usually included a train which was a requirement at court. This could be part of the dress or a separate piece, referred to as a court mantle, which was attached to the shoulders with ribbons. The evening attire would also include long gloves that extended from the bottom of the sleeves to the knuckles. A tiara or diadem could be worn in the hair as ornamentation. A simple strand of beads and dangling earrings might be worn as well.

7-C24

7-C25

7-C26

7-C27

7-C26 C. 1810

At the end of the first decade, the waistline still continues to be high but the overall dress has more structure because of the use of heavier fabrics. The dresses would have intricate patterns, borders, and ruffles. The sleeves show a series of puffs created by tying cording around the sleeve at intervals. The bonnet comes into fashion, and stays in fashion for much of the 19th century. The hairstyle is similar to the first decade.

7-C27 C. 1810

Outerwear for women included a style called a redingote or a pelisse, made of silk or light wool. In England, this was often referred to as a riding coat. The style was inspired by military coats and included a high collar and braiding and buttons across the front. It was referred to as the Brandenburg style.

7-C28

7-C29

7-C28   C. 1815

Another outerwear style popular during this time were spencer jackets. The jacket closed in the front slightly below the high waistline of the dress, with a two-part sleeve consisting of short puffy sleeves at the shoulder connected to a tighter narrow sleeve that extended to the wrist. The use of lace collars at the neckline harkens back to the Elizabethan ruffs. Neck ruffles were in vogue for the first twenty years.

7-C29   C. 1815

Evening dresses displayed more fullness in the skirt, and could have a shorter overdress open in the front, with fullness in the back. Lace trim is used to edge the dress and the sleeves. Long gloves tied at the elbow were worn with evening attire.

7-C30

7-C31

7-C30   C. 1820

In the 1820s, the waistline drops closer to the natural waistline.
The shoulders widen and the skirt is bell-shaped. The diagonal
lines on the bodice are popular trim. The walking dress includes
a parasol and bonnet, which is increasing in size and often
decorated with flowers, feathers, and bows.

7-C31   C. 1823

This is an example of an evening dress elaborately decorated with
trim. The neckline on the bodice is gathered into the center, and
then gathered into the skirt. The skirts are fuller at the hemline.
The shawl and fan are common accessories for evening wear. The
hairstyle has changed and consists of a part in the middle with
curls on the side.

7-C32

7-C33

7-C32   C. 1827

In the latter part of the decade the shoulders begin to widen, waistlines are at the natural line and the skirt is fuller. The pelisse in this image has a short cape (pelerine) attached and a lace collar at the neck. The sleeves increase in width and are referred to as leg-of-mutton sleeves. The bonnet has a wider brim with long ribbons, and the height of hat is increased because of the excessive use of trim.

7-C33   C. 1827

This walking dress has a deep V neckline, trimmed in lace with a triangular panel in the front. The width of the shoulders and hem of the dress, combined with a small waistline, gives the impression of two triangles meeting in the middle.

7-C34

7-C35

7-C34   C. 1829

The evening dresses are similar in silhouette to the day dresses. The sleeves widen with the help of puffed sleeves gathered into a band, covered by a cap sleeve that accentuates the width. The bodice gathers to the center, and the skirt is very full and festooned with garlands of bows and sometimes flowers. The skirts on ball gowns were shorter for dancing. Dancing slippers were ballet-style slippers with ribbon ties.

7-C35   C. 1830

During the decade, the dresses reach extremes in width at the shoulders and sleeves. The bodice has diagonal lines to the waist and the center triangle is made from shirred fabric. The shoulder width is accented by a tiered cape which sits on top of the sleeves. The sleeves have a larger puff sleeve above the elbow, and then a smaller one below, which gathers into a tight cuff at the wrist.

7-C36

7-C37

7-C36 C. 1834

This dress is a fine example of the extremes of the decade. The leg-of-mutton sleeves are extremely wide at the shoulder and would need support from boning or down to hold the shape. The double cape trimmed in ruffles accents the width. The front of the dress has two panels, also trimmed in ruffles. The hat sits high on the head, reminiscent of the modern fascinator, and is trimmed in feathers and flowers.

7-C37 C. 1840

In the 1840s, the waistline dips to a point below the waist. The shoulders return to a more natural line. The bodices are off the shoulder and create a V-shaped neckline. The sleeves are fitted at the top and bottom with a small puff connecting the two. It is reminiscent of sleeves during the Renaissance. Ruffles and flounces at the base on the hem are popular. The hats and headwear also return to a natural line.

7-C38

7-C39

7-C38   C. 1840

The two-piece walking outfit is introduced in this decade. The bodice is fitted, heavily corseted, and opens in the front with button closures. The sleeve is fitted to below the elbow and exposes the blouse with a ruffle. There is a small cape around the shoulders. The skirt, which has lost some of its fullness, is multi-tiered and gathers to the waistline. The bonnet follows the contour of the head and the trim is delicate.

7-C39   C. 1845

The evening dress has an off-the-shoulder bodice with a lace edge and short straight sleeves. The bodice of the dress extends to the point below the waist. The skirt is very full and falls to the floor.

7-C40

7-C41

7-C42

7-C40   C. 1822

The turban style, adopted from India, was popular during the century as a headdress for evening wear. It was usually decorated with feathers and jewels.

7-C41   C. 1827

The bonnet is a staple in headdress styles for much of the 19th century. From 1820 to the late 1830s bonnets were quite large and excessively decorated. Decorations include feathers, flowers, bows and lace.

7-C42   C. 1840

During the 1840s the bonnet returned to a more natural line with small brims and simpler trim.

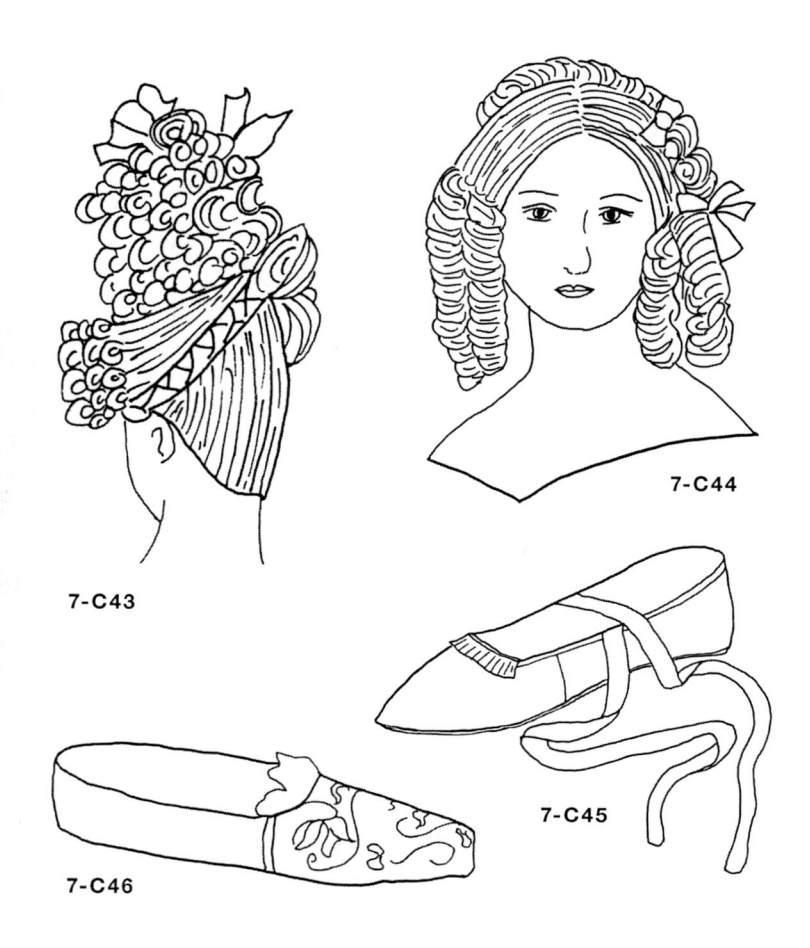

7-C43

7-C44

7-C45

7-C46

7-C43   C. 1829

Hairstyles in the early part of the century copied the Grecian style of curls piled on top of head with curls framing the face. In the 1820s, the hair styles grew higher and more ornate in response to the extremes in dress. For the evening, hair dressed in curls with ribbons and flowers piled high on the head was popular.

7-C44   C. 1845

In the 1830s and through the 1840s, the hairstyle included a part in the middle with a chignon in the back and spiral curls on the sides of the head.

7-C45   C. EARLY 19TH CENTURY

Flat-soled slippers were the popular style throughout the first half of the 19th century. They had pointed or rounded toes and were often seen with ribbons that wrapped around the ankle. The slippers with ribbon ties were referred to as dancing slippers.

7-C46   C. 1820

An example of an embroidered slipper.

Late 19th Century

The late 19th century is marked by the reign of Queen Victoria in England, who ascended the throne in 1837 and died in 1901. Known as the Victorian era, its influence extended to architecture, furniture, clothing, and the moral code of conduct. Because of advances in technology at this time, new materials and construction techniques impacted styles. This can be seen in everything from the varieties of fabric produced, the sewing machine, advances in metal as a super structure, glass, and the use of electricity.

Architecture / Furniture / Décor

Variations of style during this time period more than double. Revivalist styles go through many transitions, and begin to no longer look like the styles they represent. Companies such as the Morris Company create a "Modern Medieval" style, which attempts to focus on the purest craftsmanship techniques used in design and construction as a reaction to mass production of the Revivalist styles. A Craftsman style is also developed in the latter part of the period that attempts to devoid itself from any recognized style for both furniture and interiors, but instead allows the craft of construction to be its focus. In addition, the Art Nouveau style is developed, which reflects the flow of nature in its designs. In Chicago, a Modern style which incorporates elements of Art Nouveau and Craftsman style, coupled with tall structures, foreshadows the Modern Architectural movement in the 20th century.

Costume

The introduction of the sewing machine in 1850 has a lasting impact on the fashion industry and ready-to-wear clothing. Women's fashion is broken down into three periods: Crinoline, Bustle, and the 1890s, each with their own distinct silhouette, supported by the transitioning understructures. Men's fashion, on the other hand, begins a slow transition to the modern style of suits and coats we continue to see today. Men and women become more active in sports, and public bathing gains in popularity.

Clothing was developed specifically for these activities for practical reasons, and to be fashionable. The Victorians continue to be the inspiration behind traditional wedding attire with the princess line gowns and bustles, along with the tails and tuxedos worn by men. Photography comes of age and provides information on clothing styles not just of the upper class, but the middle and labor class as well. Actual garments and patterns, as well as paintings, give us a wide array of research opportunities.

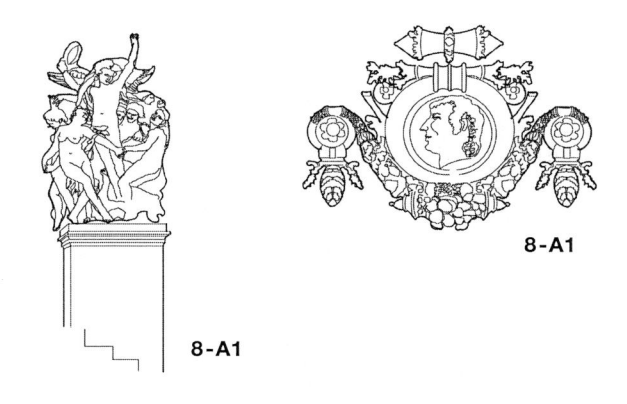

8-A1

8-A1

8-A2

8-A1   SCULPTED DETAILS OF GARNIER OPERA HOUSE
Details of the sculpted decorations for the Garnier Opera House, Paris. Represented here are the Dance sculpture by Jean-Baptiste Carpeaux, and the profile of composer Domenico Cimarosa. All are part of the Beaux-Arts Classical style. 1875.

8-A2   GARNIER OPERA HOUSE
The Garnier Opera House in Paris is in the Beaux-Arts Classical style, designed by Charles Garnier. Its style includes Roman and Classical elements such as sculptures, Corinthian columns and capitals, medallions, and numerous sculpted figures on the highest levels of the structure, accentuated in a polychrome palette. 1875.

8-A3

8-A4

8-A3   ROYAL COURTS OF JUSTICE

The Royal Courts of Justice, located in London, is in the Neo-Gothic style, designed by George Edmund Street. This style includes Gothic arched windows, steep roof lines, rose windows, and a pronounced portal main entrance in a monochrome color palette. 1882.

8-A4   PENNSYLVANIA ACADEMY OF THE FINE ARTS

The Pennsylvania Academy of the Fine Arts, designed by Frank Furness and George Hewitt, is considered in the High Gothic Revival style, although it has a number of other styles included such as Second Empire and Renaissance Revival. 1876.

8-A5

8-A6

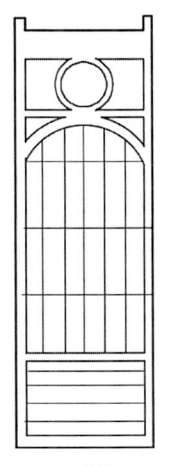

8-A7

8-A5 MARSHALL FIELD'S WHOLESALE STORE

The Marshall Field's Wholesale Store (Chicago) was designed by Henry Hobson Richardson in the Romanesque style. This style includes an exterior of rusticated stone and windows that diminish in size as it ascends to the upper floors. 1887.

8-A6 THE CRYSTAL PALACE

The Crystal Palace, designed by Joseph Paxton, was constructed of iron and glass for the Great Exhibition of 1851 in London.

8-A7 THE CRYSTAL PALACE WALL DETAIL

The wall panel made of an iron frame with glass panel inserts was designed for mass production and quick assembly.

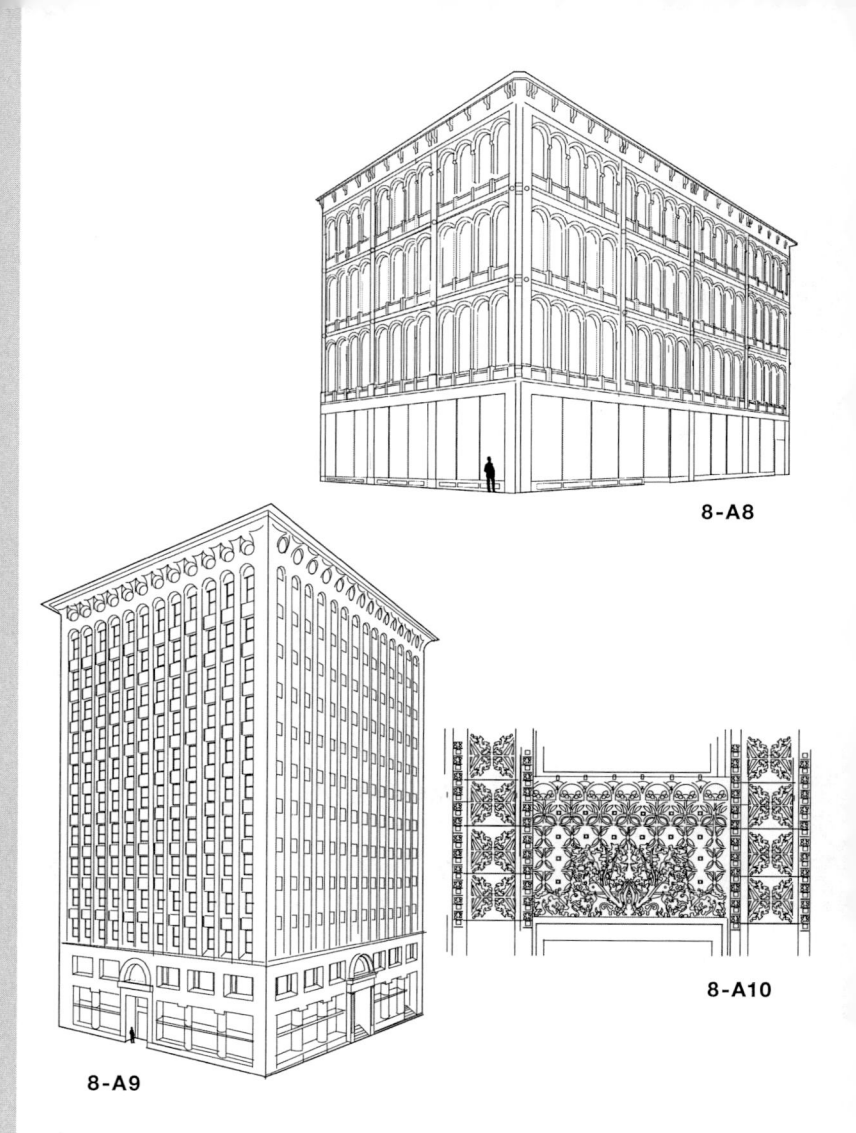

8-A8

8-A9

8-A10

8-A8 GARDNER'S WAREHOUSE

Gardner's Warehouse, Glasgow, was designed by John Baird, and is constructed of iron and glass using Classical elements for the repeated units. 1856.

8-A9 GUARANTY BUILDING

The Guaranty Building (Prudential Building) in Buffalo, New York, was designed by Louis Sullivan. It uses an iron structure and terra cotta panels to create a repeated visual theme in an Art Nouveau style. 1896.

8-A10 GUARANTY BUILDING TERRA COTTA DETAILS

Details of the terra cotta design elements include flowers and seedpods on the Guaranty Building. 1896.

8-A11

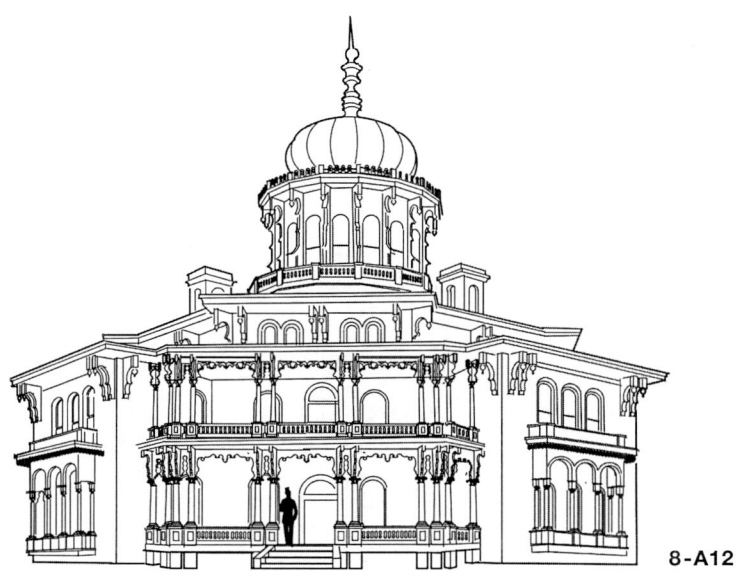

8-A12

8-A11 ITALIANATE VILLA

Morse-Libby House, located in Portland, Maine, was designed by Henry Austin in the Italianate style. Features that comprise the Italianate style include low-pitched roof, projected eaves, grouped windows, heavy hood trim to the windows, and oftentimes may have a tower. 1859.

8-A12 NUTT'S FOLLY

Longwood House, located in Natchez, Mississippi, was designed for Heller Nutt by Samuel Sloan in the Byzantine or Oriental style with an octagonal ground plan. The center cupola with onion dome was designed to draw air to the upper floors and allow light into the inner rooms. 1861.

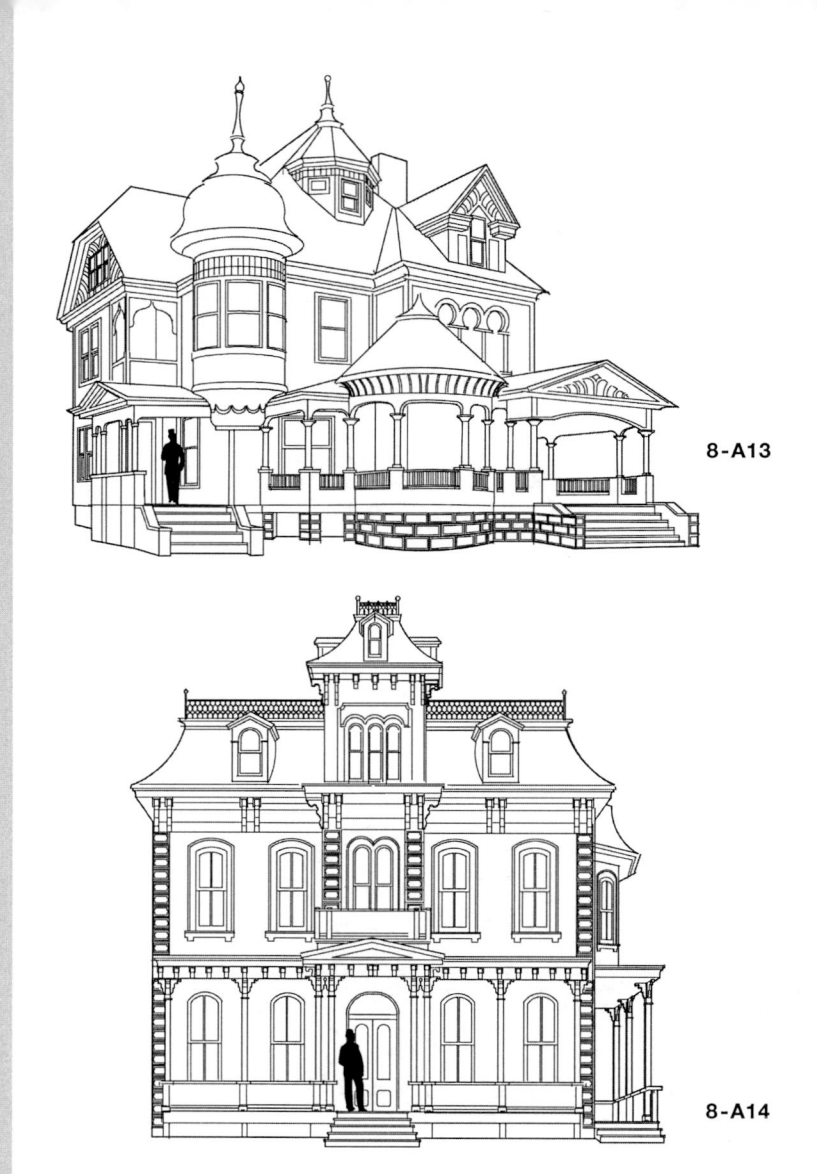

8-A13

8-A14

8-A13   PIATT-OGDEN HOUSE

The Piatt-Ogden House in Tunkhannock, Pennsylvania, was designed by George Franklin Barber for James Wilson Platt in the Queen Anne style. This style included steep roofs, wraparound porch, turret, and a second-story porch. 1896.

8-A14   SCHWARTZ HOUSE

The Schwartz House in Natchez, Mississippi is in the Second Empire style. The Second Empire style features a steep mansard roof capped off with an iron railing. This style often uses elements of the Renaissance style such as paired brackets and pronounced corner stones. 1870.

8-A15

8-A16

8-A15 ELIZABETH PLANKINTON HOUSE

Designed in the Richardsonian Romanesque style by Edward Townsend Mix, Milwaukee, it consisted of rusticated stone facade; archways over entrance, porches and windows; and towers and turrets with conical roofs. 1887.

8-A16 RED HOUSE

The Red House in Southeast London was designed by William Morris and Philip Webb and is considered in the Tudor Gothic Revival or Arts and Crafts style. The style consists of red brick, a steep red tile roof, and a variety of round arches and bull's eye windows. Window location related more to the design of each room, rather than the exterior of the structure. 1860.

8-A17

8-A18

8-A17   ISAAC BELL HOUSE

The Isaac Bell House in Newport, Rhode Island, designed by McKim, Mead and White, is considered to be in the Shingle style. This style consisted of shingle siding, wraparound porch, irregular roof lines, an open floor plan, and bamboo style columns located on the porch. 1882.

8-A18   THE CASTEL ORGEVAL HOUSE

The Castel Orgeval was designed by Hector Guimard in Villemoisson-sur-Orge, France, in the Art Nouveau style. This style consisted of flowing lines that can be found in the rounded nature of the house. It is made of local stone, with multiple rooflines and rounded arches to the windows and door openings. 1904.

8-D1

8-D2

8-D1   LYNDHURST DINING ROOM

The Lyndhurst dining room is in the High Gothic Revival style. Designed by Andrew Jackson Davis, the interior has low Gothic arches, dark red patterned wallpaper, and faux marble columns and fireplace. 1865.

8-D2   RENAISSANCE REVIVAL PARLOR

The New York parlor, designed by Augustus Truesdell, is in the Renaissance Revival style. This style is reflected in the fireplace overmantel, window valance, lighting fixtures and, to some degree, the suite of furniture in the room. 1870.

8-D3

8-D4

8-D3   ROCOCO REVIVAL PARLOR

This New York parlor is in the Rococo Revival style. The furniture of the same style is designed by John Henry Belter. The flowing naturalistic lines of the Rococo style are also reflected in the window cornice above the valance, and in the elliptical mirror above the fireplace. 1860.

8-D4   ARTS AND CRAFTS PARLOR

This interior is created in the Arts and Crafts style. Designed by Gustav Stickley, this style attempts to be devoid of decoration, but instead allows the simplistic functionality of the design to dictate its appearance. 1901.

8-D5

8-D6

8-D5 HÔTEL TASSEL STAIRCASE

The Hôtel Tassel staircase, designed by Victor Horta in Brussels, is in the Art Nouveau style. This style is reflected in the flowing natural designs in the wall paintings, floor mosaics, railings, and light fixture. The staircase is meant to look much like plants under water. 1893.

8-D6 ART NOUVEAU INTERIOR

Interior exhibited at the Exposition Universelle of Paris, designed by Louis Bigaux. The Art Nouveau style can be seen in the sweeping natural lines over the doorways, and reflected in the furniture. 1900.

8-F1

8-F2

8-F3

8-F1 GOTHIC SIDEBOARD
This sideboard in the Reformed Gothic style is designed by Bruce J. Tablert, England. This style may also be referred to as Modern Gothic, or Modern Medieval, because it incorporates many elements of the Gothic and Medieval. Displayed at the Paris Exhibition of 1867, its characteristics include incorporating elements from Gothic architecture with geometric floral images, and in the case of this piece, phrases from Shakespeare.

8-F2 RENAISSANCE REVIVAL ARMCHAIR
This armchair is in the Renaissance Revival style incorporating tufted upholstery, low-arched crest to the back with a medallion, turned pendants on the edges of the back crest and arms, and pronounced turnings on the legs. Usually constructed of dark woods. Mid to late 19th century.

8-F3 ROCOCO REVIVAL TABLE
This marble top table in the Rococo Revival style is designed by John Henry Belter. It is made of layers of rosewood laminated together. Vines, leaves, and grapes are incorporated into the surface carving. 1855.

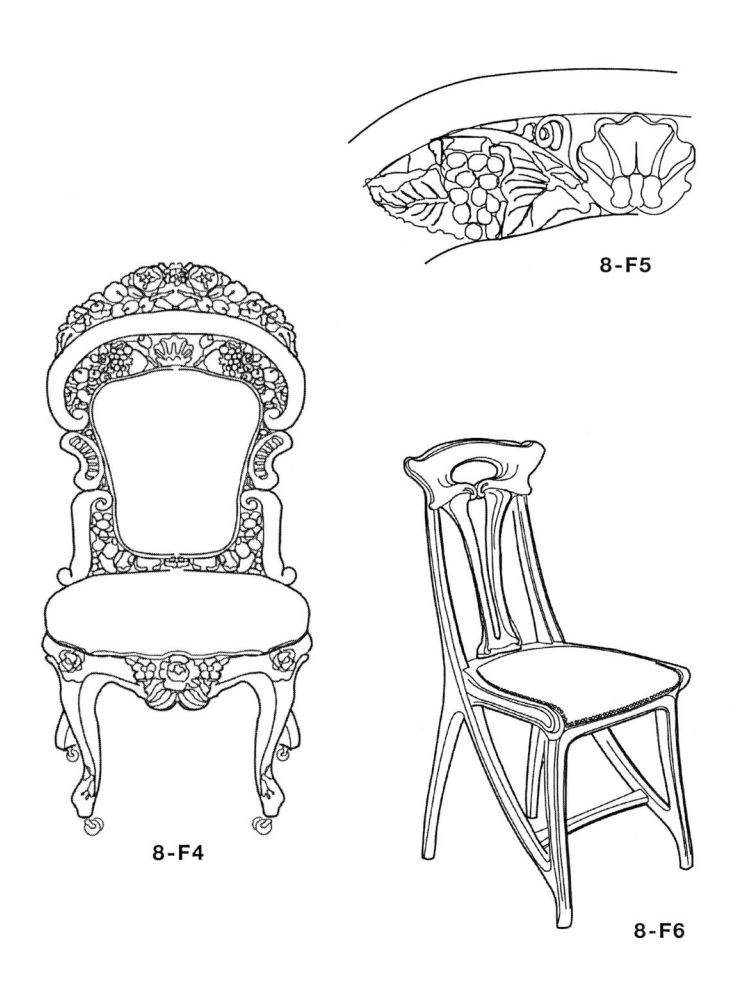

8-F5

8-F4

8-F6

8-F4   ROCOCO REVIVAL SIDE CHAIR
This side chair in the Rococo Revival style is designed by John Henry Belter. His lamination process allowed delicately carved pieces to retain more strength. The Rococo style can be seen in the vines, fruits, leaves, and seashells used in the carvings. 1860.

8-F5   DETAILS OF ROCOCO REVIVAL
Detail of the Rococo Revival side chair, designed by John Henry Belter. Because of Belter's lamination process, the carved surface could pierce the crest rail without compromising the strength of the chair. 1860.

8-F6   ART NOUVEAU SIDE CHAIR
This side chair is in the Art Nouveau style, referred to as a sleigh back shape, designed by Eugene Gaillard. Reflected in this design are the natural movement of nature, and an attempt to distance itself from the Revivalist styles.1889.

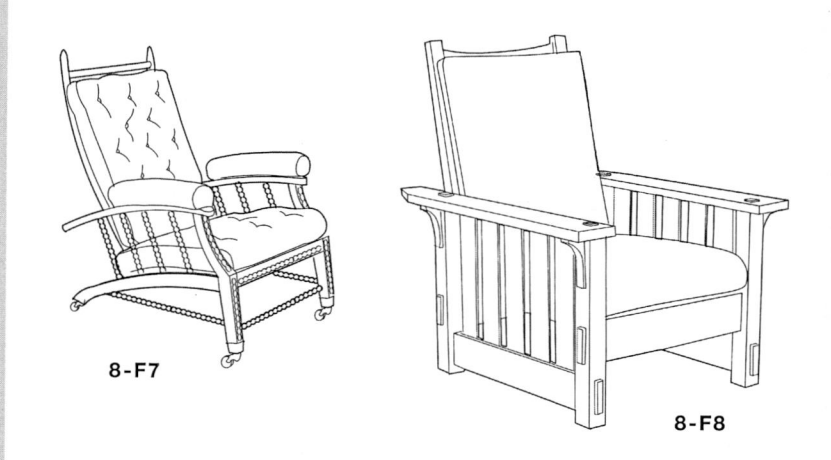

8-F7

8-F8

8-F7   MORRIS CHAIR

Although designed by Philip Webb, this chair is referred to as a
Morris chair and considered in the Arts and Crafts style. The chair
has an adjustable back and the upholstery is typical of the Morris
Company. 1870.

8-F8   MISSION STYLE ARMCHAIR

This armchair is in the Mission style, sometimes referred to as the
Craftsman style. Designed by Gustav Stickley, the style's intention
was to promote the craft aspects of fine furniture making. For this
reason the chair has no decoration, and intentionally shows the
mortise and tenon as well as dowel joints. 1902.

8-C2

8-C1

8-C3

8-C1   C. EARLY 1850S

The silhouette of the last decade continues in the early 1850's. The frock coat depicted here has a more natural shoulder line, wide lapels and fuller skirt that is seamed at the waist. The frock coat is still worn for both daywear and evening wear. Waistcoat is double-breasted, and along with the trousers provide contrast in color and pattern to the coat. Neckwear can be wide and tied into a bow. The top hat continues to be a popular choice for both day and evening wear.

8-C2   C. 1853

The frock coat becomes slimmer as the decade progresses. For evening wear, the lapels and cuffs, which were wider, could be made from velvet or other expensive and decorative fabric. The narrow bow tie is in vogue, and worn with a standing collar shirt with series of vertical pleats. You can see from the side view of this image that trousers often had a stirrup which went under the shoe. The hairstyle from the previous decade, along with the mutton chop sideburns, is still popular.

8-C3   C. 1853

The overcoat gains in popularity, and is worn over the suit underneath to protect it from the elements. The style is less fitted than the frock coat, has no waist seam, and a wider sleeve. Early on, the length of the coat mirrors the length of the frock coat underneath. The top hat, gloves, and walking stick are popular accessories for men.

8-C4

8-C5

8-C6

8-C4   C. 1853

The tailcoat had wider lapels during this decade, and the front of the coat dips below the waist, following the line of the waistcoat. For evening or formal occasions, a white waistcoat and bow tie were required. Shirts had a standing collar and vertical ruffles or pleats. We still see this style in the present day at formal events.

8-C5   C. 1856

By mid-decade the frock coat was slimmer and the collar and lapels were smaller in size. The coat buttoned higher. The trousers are more relaxed and no longer have stirrups.

8-C6   C. 1859

The sack suit appeared at the end of the decade and was the forerunner of the modern suit. The waist seam is gone, the sleeves are wider, and the overall silhouette is boxy. Often the trousers and coat would match, and the waistcoat would provide a bit of color and pattern. This look was popular for daywear. The low flat crown hat with medium size brim was popular for casual wear, and made out of straw for summer.

8-C8

8-C7

8-C9

8-C7   C. 1860

The overcoats in the 1860s begin to resemble the modern-day overcoat or Chesterfield. The coat has a vertical silhouette without a waist seam, and is longer than previous decade.

8-C8   C. 1861

The Inverness cape consisted of a combination of a long and short cape with a small collar often made of velvet. This would be worn with gloves, along with a top hat and walking stick.

8-C9   C. 1863

In the 1860s, the sack coat becomes slimmer, shorter and has a smaller collar. The waistcoat buttons higher and is worn with a simple ascot. "Ditto suits" in which all the pieces of a suit are of the same fabric and color become popular, much like the modern suit. The bowler hat, with its rounded crown and narrow brim, is introduced during the 1860s and is worn with day or casual wear.

8-C10

8-C11

8-C12

8-C10   C. 1866

By the mid 1860s the frock coat is shorter in length, very straight in line, and has a small collar. It was the fashion for men to button the top button only during this period. It is still seamed at the waist, and follows the silhouette of the sack coat.

8-C11   C. 1870

The suit coat makes its appearance in the 1870s. This coat is shorter and straighter in line than the sack coat, and has a shawl collar and hip pockets. It buttons high on the chest and reveals only a small edge of the waistcoat. The shirt has a detached turnover collar which was popular for casual or daywear. The four-in-hand tie, resembling the modern tie, gains in popularity.

8-C12   C. 1870

This suit, which would be worn for business attire, has a single-breasted waistcoat that buttons high with a four-in-hand tie. He is wearing gloves, top hat, and walking stick.

8-C13

8-C15

8-C14

8-C13 & 8-C14   C. 1873

These two illustrations reflect lounging attire for men of the period and worn for informal occasions at home. The longer lounging coat, 8-C13, with the shawl collar and belt with tassels, and the smoking jacket, 8-C14, with shawl collar were made from luxurious fabrics such as satin, silk, or brocades. The chain for the pocket watch is visible on the waistcoat for the smoking jacket.

8-C15   C. 1882

The cutaway coat, also known as a morning coat, gains in popularity for daywear or business attire. There is a seam that sits below the natural waistline, and the lower section of coat curves to the back. The coat buttons to mid-chest allowing the high-buttoned waistcoat to be seen. The shirt has a standing collar and bow tie. The trousers are slimmer than the previous decade and could be checked or striped. He wears a bowler and gloves, and carries a walking stick.

8-C16

8-C17

8-C18

8-C16   C. 1882

The suit coat has a curved front which differentiates it from the sack suit during the same period with the straight square edges. It closed high on the neck with only the top button closed, revealing the bottom of the waistcoat. Collars were very small. This model has patch pockets at chest and hipline. Hairstyle for men was closely cropped and clean shaven, although small mustaches were still popular.

8-C17   C. 1882

Another style of suit coat with a notched collar and double pockets at the hip line. The coat buttons all the way down, hiding the waistcoat.

8-C18   C. 1882

The Chesterfield overcoat is knee length, cut straight, and has a fly opening in center front. He carries an umbrella and wears gloves and a top hat.

8-C20

8-C19

8-C21

8-C19   C. 1882

The frock coat continues to be worn for daywear or formal occasions, such as weddings and funerals, until the early 20th century. The coat still has the signature waist seam connecting the upper and lower coat. The silhouette is vertical and can be single or double breasted, buttoning high on the neck. It is usually worn with a white waistcoat, striped trousers, silk top hat, and gloves.

8-C20   C. 1892

This sack suit has a straight square look but is slimmer than in the 1880s. It is double-breasted with multiple pockets at the hip line, and a wide notched collar. The shirt has a standing collar with a four-in-hand tie. The trousers are fuller and he wears a straw boater, which had a low crown with a hat band, and medium size horizontal brim.

8-C21   C. 1893

The suit coat has a slimmer silhouette, curved front, and buttons lower on the chest than previous decade. The trousers and jacket often match with contrast provided by the waistcoat. A bowler, gloves, and walking stick finish the look.

8-C22

8-C23

8-C24

8-C22   C. 1893

The cutaway coat has a waist seam and is longer in the back, reaching just above the knees. The coat buttons lower in front, revealing the waistcoat which could be single or double-breasted and usually showed off a watch chain. The shirt in this illustration has a wing tip collar. This morning coat was often worn with striped trousers, and can still be seen occasionally as wedding attire.

8-C23   C. 1895

Tails are worn strictly for evening or formal wear. As of the 1870s they could be worn with either a matching black or white waistcoat, but white was still worn for formal occasions. Both the coat and waistcoat are open much lower in the front. The shirt would be white and have either a standing or wing tip collar, and worn with a bowtie.

8-C24   C. 1899

The white dinner jacket is in vogue from the late 1880s through the mid 20th century as evening attire, however the tailcoat was still required for formal occasions. The jacket was worn with black trousers and a waistcoat that was cut low in front. The white shirt would have a standing, or wing tip collar, and worn with a bow tie, which is usually black.

8-C25

8-C26

8-C27

8-C25   C. 1899

Suits at the end of the decade are shorter and button lower in the front. The single-breasted suits still curved from front to back. The collars are wider than in the earlier decade. Waistcoats which could be single or double-breasted still buttoned high and could be seen when the jacket was closed. Trousers were slimmer, had a button-fly front, and could have a crease down the front which became popular during this decade.

8-C26   C. 1899

This double-breasted suit has noticeably wide lapels both on the jacket and waistcoat. It is shorter than the earlier part of the decade, and buttons lower in the front revealing the upper part of the waistcoat. He is wearing a fedora which came into favor in the late 19th century. This wool felt hat has a crease in the top with a snap brim. It was similar in style to the homburg.

8-C27   C. 1898

Sportswear fashion was popular with both men and women in the late 19th century. For men the knickers, which were full short trousers that fastened below the knee and were worn over hose and either short boots or shoes for many sports. This was combined with a shirt, tie or ascot, waistcoat, and jacket. This particular style was worn when golfing and includes a cap that matches the plaid pattern in the knickers.

8-C29

8-C28

8-C30

8-C28　C. 1898

The Norfolk Jacket became popular in the 1880s for hunting, as well as other sports, such as cycling and golfing. It is single-breasted, and characterized by the box pleats on the front and back and is belted. It is often worn with matching knickers for sporting attire, but could be worn with trousers for casual wear. This style is popular into the beginning of the 20th century.

8-C29　C. 1891

A double-breasted formal waistcoat with shawl collar and welt pockets. The white shirt has a wing tip collar and it is being worn with a bowtie. The waistcoat would be either black or white and often have satin lapels.

8-C30　C. 1894

The single-breasted waistcoat buttons to the mid-chest and is worn with a shirt with a standing collar and a bowtie. This would be worn under the coat for business and casual attire. The vest has two sets of welt pockets at chest and waist.

8-C32

8-C31

8-C33

8-C31   C. 1894

The double-breasted waistcoat has a notched collar with a wide lapel similar to coat lapels and worn for business or casual attire. The shirt has a standing collar and the cuffs were closed with cuff links. Ascots were popular neckwear for daytime, casual dress, or sporting in the late 19th century. Men styled their short hair with a center part. Mustaches were still in vogue.

8-C32   C. 1866

This is an example of a bowler hat that was introduced in the 1860s, and shared popularity with the top hat. It was the early form of the derby, which continued to be popular in the early 20th century. It had a hard-rounded crown and a narrow brim with a band, and usually made of wool felt. We also see a closeup of the mutton chop sideburns which were popular in the early Victorian period.

8-C33   C. 1866

The top hat continued to be the most popular hat of the 19th century and was worn both with daytime and evening attire. In the later 19th century the crown was lower. The top hat was made of wool, or silk, and continued to be worn in the 20th century for formal occasions.

8-C34

8-C35

8-C36

8-C37

8-C34   C. 1860S
Short leather boot had a cap toe and elastic insets that allowed the style of the shoe to be smooth without visible fastenings. The stacked heel was 1.25". These were worn with suits for daytime, sports or casual wear.

8-C35   C. 1885
Black patent leather shoe with an elastic insert allowed for the shoes to be slipped on, while the lacing was for decoration only. Shoes were slim and had a 1" stacked heel. These could be worn with spats, which was fashionable.

8-C36   C. 1888
Black leather Balmoral boot with square cap toe and 1.25" heel. Boots no longer has elastic insets and laced up the front.

8-C37   C. 1900
By end of century the oxford shoe came into favor and continued into the 20th century. This oxford brogue had a winged cap and 1.25" stacked heel.

8-C38

8-C39

8-C38 C. 1852

The Crinoline period dominated women's fashion of the 1850s until the mid 1860s. The skirts had a wide bell-shaped line with a fitted bodice. The bonnet was worn further back on head revealing more of the hair. The cape is created by multiple flounces and has a flat lace collar. Capes were the most popular style for women's outerwear and they continued in fashion through the end of the century.

8-C39 C. 1852

Evening dress with graduated ruffles on the underskirt and a scalloped overskirt is reminiscent of evening dresses from the late 18th century. For evening wear, the bodice was wide, and off the shoulder, with short sleeves. The hairstyle is pulled to the back of the neck and decorated with flowers and ribbons.

8-C40

8-C41

8-C40   C. 1858

In the mid 1850s, the crinoline or hooped petticoat was introduced to support the widening girth of the skirts. See 8-C62 for a close look at the crinoline structure. This day dress from later in the decade shows the bell-shaped skirt composed of a series of flounces. The bodice has rounded shoulders and a series of tucks/pleats that radiate to the center point which sits below the natural waistline. The pagoda sleeve, an open sleeve that flared below the elbow, reveals the sleeve of the chemise underneath.

8-C41   C. 1860

By the 1860s, the skirt sits at the natural waistline, with two layers of lace embellishing the lower part of dress. The fitted bodice, trimmed in lace, has a high neckline that buttons down the front. The sleeves are fitted, and decorated with two layers of lace. Lace remains popular on garments throughout the remainder of the century.

8-C42

8-C43

8-C42   C. 1862

This day ensemble includes the wide bell-shaped skirt, fitted bodice that buttons down the front. It is worn with a bolero jacket which comes back into fashion in the 1860s. The jacket and skirt are trimmed in braid, a popular trim throughout the late 19th century. Hat, parasol, and gloves are standard accessories for daytime.

8-C43   C. 1863

This two-piece day outfit has a skirt and a tailored semi-fitted coat with a flat collar edged in lace and full sleeves. In the 1860s, the skirts increased in width, with the extra fabric pleated into the waistband. The front of the skirt becomes flatter, and the back of the dress becomes much fuller as fashion transitions into the bustle style. The bonnets are close fitting to the head with a very small brim.

8-C45

8-C44

8-C44   C. 1866

This evening dress illustrates the beginning of the bustle silhouette that dominates the next two decades. The skirt has a cone-shaped silhouette and flat front. The overskirt with ruffled edge emphasizes the fullness in the back of the dress. We saw a similar silhouette at the end of the 17th century. The decorative swags of fabric on the lower half of the dress and ruffled edge are similar to the ball gowns of the late 18th century. The bodice sits at the natural waistline and has a wide neckline similar to the previous decade.

8-C45   C. 1870

This two-piece outfit has a full skirt, with a bustle in back. From the side view you can see the flattened front silhouette in contrast to the fullness in the back. See 8-C63 for a close look at the bustle structure. The bodice has a standing collar, and fastens in the front to the waistline. The overdress does not have a waist seam and drapes over the bustle in the back. The hair is pulled up with more height than previous period.

8-C46

8-C47

8-C46   C. 1873

As we move into the middle of the 1870s, the line is more vertical. The skirt is now slim with fullness created by the series of gathered fabric and ruffles on the bottom half of skirt. The bustle overskirt is quite elaborate, and creates a train in the back of the dress. The bustle effect is still used in modern bridal dresses. The bodice front extends below the waist to a deep point emphasizing the overall vertical line. For evening the bare shoulder and short puffed sleeves were still popular. The hair is piled high on the head and decorated with curls.

8-C47   C. 1874

This day outfit reflects the reduction in width of the overall skirt and the increased emphasis on the back of the dress. The overskirt creates an apron effect in the front with the folds of fabric gathered and pulled up in the back to create the bustle. This bears similarity to the Polonaise style in the 18th century. The hat, with a small upturned brim, perches on top of the hair.

8-C48

8-C49

8-C48   C. 1881

In the later bustle period, the bodice extends to the hipline creating a cuirass bodice. The bodice has a natural shoulder line, slight V-shaped neckline, and fitted sleeves. Braided trim is evident on the front of the bodice. The skirt is at the narrowest point, and at times hindered movement. The overskirt, which is folded and pleated to create a diagonal line, still drapes around the underskirt, creating some fullness in the back.

8-C49   C. 1882

A back view of a day dress showing the bodice, which extends below the waistline and dips deep in the back center, mirroring the front. The sleeves are fitted and adorned with a flower. The skirt is narrow, and the overskirt is pulled across the front in a series of folds, and gathered in the back to create the bustled effect.

8-C50

8-C51

8-C50   C. 1882

This evening dress has a deep V neckline on the bodice which is edged in lace and has an added bow for modesty. The lower part of bodice extends to a deep point below the waist. The skirt has a series of gathered and ruffled fabric but still maintains the tubular silhouette of the time. The overskirt is gathered into a soft bustle in the back. Elbow-length gloves were worn with evening attire.

8-C51   C. 1885

The side view of the dress shows us an example of the more extreme bustle silhouette. The front of skirt is flat, the overskirt which extends low in the front, is drawn up high in back in folds to create the bustle which extends horizontal from the waist. The jacket is edged in a series of ruffles that help to accentuate the bustled look.

8-C52

8-C53

8-C52 C. 1886

After 1885, the bustle starts to lose its popularity, and the silhouette become softer and more natural. This evening dress has some of the elements of the previous style, such as the overskirt and long train, but it illustrates a more natural line. An asymmetrical or diagonal line is seen on the overskirt. The bodice has a square neckline, short sleeves, and dips slightly below the waistline in front. Long gloves, a fan, and a feather in the hair finish the look.

8-C53 C. 1888

By the late 1880s, daywear had a more tailored look, with less ruffles and flounces. The jacket has wide lapels, fitted sleeves with cuffs, and a diagonal line which is echoed in the overskirt below. A blouse with a standing collar is worn under the jacket. The folds in the overskirt create swags in the front, and there is a small nod to the bustle in back. The bonnet sits higher on the head accommodating the hairstyle.

8-C55

8-C54

8-C54   C. 1891

This tea dress illustrates the simplicity of line at the beginning of the 1890s. The dress has a fitted bodice with a small waist, and the skirt drapes in soft folds from the hip to the floor. The sleeves, which are a focal point during this decade, begin to increase in fullness to below the elbow, and gather into a tight-fitting lower sleeve. A long sleeveless robe with a train is worn over the dress. The high neckline is finished with an inset of ruffled lace.

8-C55   C. 1896

The middle of the decade saw extremes in fashion. The bodice shows the return of the leg-of-mutton sleeves from earlier in the century. The shoulders are broad, the waistline is small, and the conical-shaped skirt is reminiscent of the hourglass figure of the Romantic period. The jacket is decorated with a series of decorative braiding and sports a peplum that evokes the style of military jackets. The standing collar with ruffle is similar in style to the jabot of the 18th century. Hats with wide brims trimmed with large feathers became popular.

233

8-C56

8-C57

8-C56   C. 1896

This evening dress is paired with a short bolero jacket with a scalloped edge and trimmed in ruffles. The sleeves, which are extremely large, are referred to as balloon sleeves. The bodice has diagonal folds and the skirt is conical in shape with a wide waistband. Long gloves and flower corsages were popular accessories for evening wear. The hair was dressed high on the head and adorned with flowers or feathers.

8-C57   C. 1897

This day dress shows a gradual decrease in the upper part of the sleeves, but there is still a broad-shouldered look enhanced by wings over the top of the sleeves. The bodice of the dress has a square neckline topped with a high-collared insert trimmed in ruffles, resembling the ruff of the Elizabethan period. The lower ruffle of the dress was often tacked up, showing off the petticoat in complimentary colors and patterns.

8-C59

8-C58

8-C58   C. 1897

The evening wear also reflects the decrease in sleeve width and
the natural line of the second half of the decade. The bodice has a
square neckline, and extends slightly below the waist. A diamond-
shaped pattern in the center of the bodice is created by contrasting
fabrics edged in trim. The skirt has a smooth flat front, with excess
fabric gathered into folds in the back, that extend into a train. The
hair is piled high on the head with a feather for decoration.

8-C59   C. 1898

As women enter the workforce in larger numbers the three-piece
suit makes its appearance. The jacket was fitted and extended
below the waist, with only a small amount of fullness at the top of
the sleeve. Under the jacket the woman wore a vest with lapels,
similar in line to the men's style. The blouse was full and gathered
into the high-standing collar. The skirt still maintained the A-line
shape but with less structure. This style continues into the early
part of the 1900s.

8-C60

8-C61

8-C60   C. 1895

This lawn tennis dress illustrates the fashion trend of mid 1890s, with the increase in the size of the upper sleeves, along with a structured A line skirt with box pleats, which sits at the natural waist. The blouse gathers into the high standing collar. The straw boater hat was popular with both women and men during the late 19th century.

8-C61   C. 1897

This bicycle suit, as it was called, consisted of a short jacket, collared blouse and tie, and bloomers or knickerbockers, which were very full breeches, gathered into a waistband. Bloomers were introduced by Amelia Bloomer in 1851 but the fashion trend did not catch on until later in the century when they became a staple in cycling and bathing suit attire. Hose was worn along with short boots and spats.

8-C62

8-C63

8-C62   C. 1850S

The crinoline cage was introduced in the mid 1850s and helped to support the very wide skirts that were the style during this time. Prior to this, women wore multiple petticoats with ruffles under the skirt. The new style was lighter, and made of whalebone or steel inserted into casings. It would be worn over a chemise and petticoat to protect the skin.

8-C63   C. 1870S

The bustle style needed a new understructure that would support the fullness at the back of the dress, while maintaining a flat front. In this example, steel wires are inserted into the casings of the bustle made of cotton. It is worn with a chemise, corset, and drawers.

8-C64

8-C65

8-C66

8-C64   C. 1864

An example of a small summer hat that tilted over the forehead, and was trimmed with flowers, feathers, and bows. It was a style favored by the Empress Eugenie, wife of Napoleon III.

8-C65   C. 1889

The bonnet stays in favor throughout the century. In the later part of the Victorian era, the brim regains its prominence, and the crown sits high on the head accommodating the height of the hairstyle.

8-C66   C. 1897

The hats at the end of the century had wide straight brims and low crowns, but were well decorated with bows, flowers and feathers. They tended to perch on top of the hair which was pulled up high on the head.

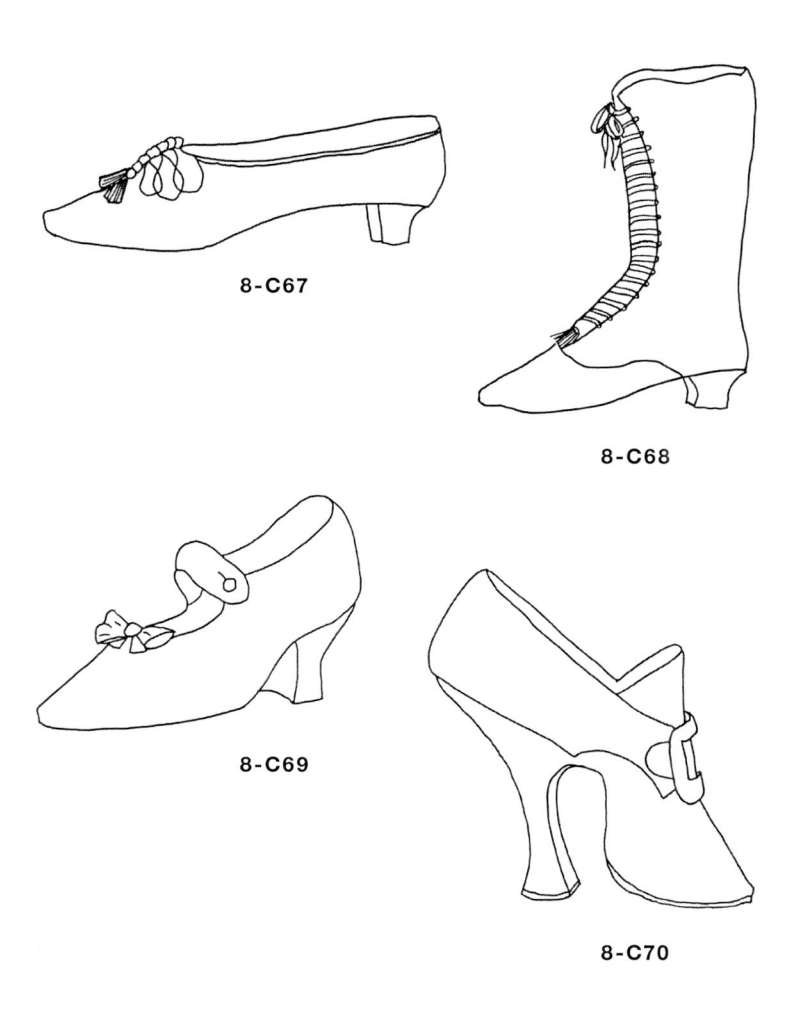

8-C67

8-C68

8-C69

8-C70

8-C67   C. 1864
Slipper shoe with a small heel popular during the mid century for evening attire.

8-C68   C. 1864
Leather boot, which would have been worn for daytime or sporting attire. It laced up the front.

8-C69   C. LATE 19TH CENTURY
This dress shoe has a higher heel and strap with a button closure and trimmed in a bow. It would have been worn for evening or formal occasions.

8-C70   C. 1890
In the 1890s, a Cromwell shoe with a 5" heel gained popularity.

KATHLEEN DONNELLY received her Bachelor's Degree in Speech and Theatre from the State University of New York at Oneonta, and her Master of Fine Arts Degree in Theatre Design from Northwestern University in Evanston, Illinois. Before moving to Oshkosh in 1995, she designed costumes and lighting for universities and theatre companies in the New York City area, including: Skyboat Road Company, Long Island Theatre Company, Riverside Shakespeare, and the Forum Theatre in New Jersey. She is an Associate Professor Emerita at the University of Wisconsin Oshkosh and has taught courses in Design, History of Styles, Stage Management, Costume Construction and Makeup. She is the past Chair of Design, Technology & Management for the Kennedy Center American College Theatre Festival, Region III, and was awarded the Kennedy Center Gold Medallion in 2017. She also served as chair of the USITT Midwest Regional Section, and currently serves in the position of Vice-Commissioner of Expo and Exhibits for the USITT Costume Commission.

ROY HOGLUND received his Bachelor's Degree in Studio Art from the University of Wisconsin Oshkosh, and his Master of Fine Arts Degree in Design for the Stage from the University of Washington in Seattle. He is Professor Emeritus at the University of Wisconsin Oshkosh. Prior to his work with UW Oshkosh, he was an Associate Professor with the University of New Mexico in Albuquerque. Since he began teaching at UW Oshkosh in 1986, his responsibilities have included teaching Design, History of Styles, Scenic Painting, Stage Management, and various technical courses as well as designing lighting and scenery academically and professionally at Seattle Repertory Theatre, Albuquerque Civic Light Opera, Santa Fe Festival Theatre, and New American Theatre. He helped create and coordinate Design Storm at the Kennedy Center American College Theatre Festival Region III, served as chair of the USITT Midwest Regional Section, and created the *Technical Source Guide* through the USITT Technical Production Commission, originally published through *Sightlines*.